ESSAY ON THE PAHLAVI LANGUAGE

ESSAY ON THE PAHLAVI LANGUAGE

MARTIN HAUG

GYAN

Published by

Gyan Publishing House
5, Ansari Road
Daryaganj, New Delhi-110002
Phone: 011-47034999, 9811692060
E-mail: books@gyanbooks.com

Distribution Network
gyanbooks.com
India, USA, Canada, UK, Australia

ISBN: 978-93-7316-126-6 (PB)

First Published, 1870

2nd Impression 2025

Printed at: Gyan Press, Delhi.

ESSAY ON THE PAHLAVI LANGUAGE
Author: MARTIN HAUG

ESSAY

ON

THE PAHLAVI LANGUAGE

BY

MARTIN HAUG, Ph. D.,

PROFESSOR OF SANSCRIT AND COMPARATIVE PHILOLOGY AT THE UNIVERSITY OF MUNICH,
MEMBER OF THE ROYAL BAVARIAN ACADEMY OF SCIENCES, ETC. ETC.

[FROM THE PAHLAVI-PAZAND GLOSSARY EDITED BY DESTUR HOSHANGJI AND M. HAUG.]

STUTTGART.

PRINTED AT THE K. HOFBUCHDRUCKEREI ZU GUTTENBERG
(CARL GRÜNINGER).

1870.

TO

MARC JOSEPH MÜLLER, Ph. D.,

PROFESSOR OF ORIENTAL LANGUAGES AT THE UNIVERSITY OF MUNICH, MEMBER OF THE ROYAL BAVARIAN ACADEMY OF SCIENCES ETC. ETC., FOUNDER OF A SCIENTIFIC INVESTIGATION INTO THE PAHLAVI LANGUAGE IN EUROPE,

THIS ESSAY IS INSCRIBED AS A TOKEN OF FRIENDSHIP AND HIGH ESTEEM

BY THE

AUTHOR.

The Pahlavî language is one of the most enigmatical languages known to have existed. Its nature is difficult to determine, since it exhibits itself, at first sight, as a very curious mixture of Semitic and Iranian elements; its origin and especially the age which gave rise to it, are enshrouded in darkness. Although it is well known that it was used as the official language of the Sasanian kings (A. D. 266—640), as appears from inscriptions on coins and rocks, and though there still exist many works, connected with the Zoroastrian religion, which are written in this language, yet we are still left in the dark as to the causes which led the Iranian kings to adopt such a strange language for their official communications, and induced the priests to use it in their commentaries on the sacred books.

Like other languages, the Pahlavî as the official language of a once mighty empire, which struck terror into the Roman and Byzantine emperors, has been made a subject of study by some European scholars; but their efforts to unravel the mysteries of this idiom, have been rewarded as yet with but little success. Even the inscriptions of Assyria and Babylonia, though handed down to us in a very complicated and cumbrous system of writing, have been read and partly deciphered, before we have succeeded in understanding even the general sense of a single

Pahlavî inscription of any length, which has not a Greek translation attached to it, although the alphabet was known, and a knowledge of the Iranian, as well as the Semitic, elements of the Pahlavî was easily obtainable. It has even been doubted whether the language used in the inscriptions is the same as that we find employed in the books; and some scholars have considered the Pahlavî as a very odd mixture of different linguistic elements, such as Persian, Afghanic, Armenian and Chaldee, and have thereby made 'confusion worse confounded'.

The chief reasons why the results hitherto obtained have proved so little satisfactory to thoughtful scholars, have been first, the difficulty of the subject, arising from the ambiguous Pahlavî writing and the strange character of the idiom; secondly, the want of sufficient available material; and thirdly, the circumstance that the few scholars who took any interest in Pahlavî, were divided into two parties, one of which investigated only the meagre legends on coins, whilst the other was almost exclusively engaged on the Pahlavî of the books, without studying the inscriptions.

In the following pages, I shall endeavour to determine the true character and nature of the Pahlavî language, and to fix the age in which it may have originated, by availing myself of all the materials at my disposal, of the inscriptions as well as of the books, and especially by making an attempt at deciphering the Sasanian inscriptions. Before entering however, upon the proper subject of this essay, I shall give a short sketch of all that has been written in Europe regarding Pahlavì, with occasional critical remarks on some of the principal works on the subject, chiefly for the benefit of young Pahlavî students among the Parsi community.

1. History of the researches made in Europe into the Pahlavî language and literature.

The first European who possessed some knowledge of Pahlavî, was A n q u e t i l D u p e r r o n, the celebrated Frenchman who first made Europe acquainted with the sacred books of the Zoroastrians. Even before he gave the learned world his translation of the Z e n d - a v e s t a, he published (in 1768) two memoirs in the Mémoires de l'Académie des inscriptions [1]), forming an essay on the ancient languages of Persia, in which he made known the Zand and Pahlavî alphabets. He stated the number of characters in the latter to be twenty-four, but he gave no account of the language itself. In his 'Zend-avesta' (Paris 1771, vol. III. pag. 343 — 422) he published a translation of a whole work written in Pahlavî, the so-called Bundehesh, which is a collection of various fragments on cosmogony, cosmography, mythology and legendary history; this translation was accompanied by a facsimile of the first nineteen lines of the Paris MS. of the work, with a transliteration into the Roman character and a translation of them. In the same volume (pag. 476 — 526) he also printed a Pahlavî-Pâzand vocabulary in Roman characters, which is the same as that published in the present work; but the original arrangement in chapters was disregarded, and the order of the Persian alphabet introduced, to the great disadvantage of the vocabulary.

Anquetil made no attempt at deciphering or explaining any of the Pahlavî inscriptions, and was so little acquainted with the writing, that he declared the Pahlavî inscriptions, which are found in the caves of Kanheri near Bombay, to be Mongolic.

The honour of having laid the first foundation in deciphering the Sasanian inscriptions on rocks and coins, belongs to Sylvestre de Sacy, one of the most eminent oriental scholars who ever lived. His 'Mémoires sur diverses antiquités de la Perse' (Paris, 1793) form an epoch as regards the study of the monuments and coins of ancient Persia. The work in question contains five memoirs. In the first, he treats of the monuments and Pahlavî inscriptions which are found at Naksh-i Rustam, where there are two short Greek inscriptions accompanied by inscriptions in two kinds of Pahlavî character [2]). Incorrect copies of these inscriptions,

---

1) Tome XXXI. pag. 339 — 442. Both memoirs had been read before the Academy in 1763.

2) See Flandin, Voyage en Perse vol. IV. pl. 181ter.

made by **Chardin** and **Sam. Flower**, existed already before the time of **Niebuhr**, to whom we are indebted for the first transcript of them which was sufficiently accurate to make a decipherment possible. De Sacy compared all these copies carefully, and arrived at the conclusion that there existed only two Greek inscriptions, and that those communicated by Chardin, Flower and Niebuhr were identical. Dr. **Hyde**, the celebrated author of 'Historia religionis veterum Persarum' (1700), had already made an attempt at explaining the Greek text, but had signally failed. He had read *ΑΡΤΑΞΑΡΟΥ* as *ΑΛΕΞΑΝΔΡΟΥ*, and consequently referred the whole inscription to Alexander the Great 1). De Sacy showed that this reading was incorrect, and that the king mentioned in the inscription was Ardeshîr *(Artakhshatr)*, the founder of the Sasanian dynasty. After having restored the Greek text in a critical manner, he made it the starting-point for deciphering one of the two texts in oriental characters, as he believed their contents to be the same. He was successful beyond expectation in his attempt, and thus laid a solid foundation for all future decipherments 2). In a similar attempt upon the other oriental text, he was however much less successful. Although he had Greek translations at his disposal, the task was by no means an easy one, as nothing at all

1) See Hist. de relig. vet. Pers. 1st edition, pag. 519—520.

2) The following are the Greek and one of the Pahlavî texts of one of the inscriptions at Naksh-i Rustam. The small Greek letters indicate those which are defective in the original, as appears from the copy in Fland. voy. en Perse, vol. 4, pl. 181ter; and the letters *E*, *Σ* and *Ω* are formed like *ε*, *c* and *ω*, in the original.

ΤΟΥΤΟ ΤΟ πΡΟΣΟΠΟΝ ΜΑΣΔΑΣΝΟΥ
ΘΕΟΥ ΑΡΤΑξαϱΟΥ ΒΑΣΙΛΕΟΣ ΒΑΣΙΛΕΩΝ
ΑΡΙΑΝΩΝ εκγενΟΥΣ ΘΕΩΝ ΥΙΟΥ
ΘΕΟΥ ΠΑΠΑκΟΥ ΒΑΣΙΛΕΩΣ

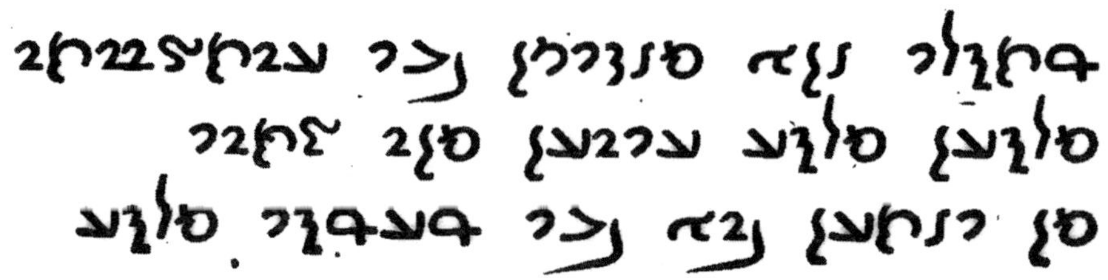

was known of Pahlavî, except the scanty and uncritical notices and remarks to be found in Anquetil's works.

In his third memoir, he applied the results thus obtained (which however explained only a few names and titles) to the elucidation of the legends on some of the Sasanian coins, as he found the characters and most of the words were identical with those at Naksh-i Rustam. He read on them correctly the names of Ardeshîr (*Artakhshatr*), Shâpûr (*Shahpûhrî*), Behrâm (*Varahrân*) and Hormazd (*Aûharmazdî*); but his other readings of names were doubtful, or erroneous. In his fourth memoir, he also succeeded in explaining the Pahlavî inscriptions of *Kirmanshah* or *Bisutun*, with the exception of their commencements.

In a subsequent 'Mémoire sur les monumens et les inscriptions de Kirmanschah ou Bisoutoun, et sur divers autres monumens Sassanidès' (1815) [1]), he corrected some of his previous mistakes. The results published by him, in his various memoirs, have formed the basis on which all subsequent investigations have been founded.

The first who applied these results to further researches, was Sir W. Ouseley, in his 'Observations on some medals and gems, bearing inscriptions in the Pahlavî or ancient Persick character' (London, 1801.) By means of De Sacy's discoveries, he was able to read the legends on about 23 silver coins in the Hunterian Museum, containing names already known; but the only addition he made to our knowledge of Pahlavî, was

---

Transliteration of the Pahlavî text.

Patkalî zanman mazdayasn bagî Artakhshatr,
malkân malkâ Aîrân, minû chitrî
min yaztân, barman bagî Pâpakî malkâ.

Translation.

The image, this, of the Mazda-worshipping, divine Artakhshatr, king of the kings of Aîrân, of spiritual origin from God, son of the divine Pâpakî, the king.

1) In the 'Mémoires de l'Institut Royal de France, classe d'histoire', tome II. pag. 162—242.

by reading, for the first time, the name of Khosru (*khûslûî*) on certain coins.

J. C. Tychsen of Göttingen also published some articles on the Sasanian coins [1]), but he made no advance whatever; all he could do, was to apply the results obtained by De Sacy, and venture on some guesses.

For a long time no scholar directed his attention to Pahlavî; the learned world seemed to rest satisfied with the labors of Anquetil Duperron and Sylvestre de Sacy.

Twenty-four years after their last publication on the subject (De Sacy's final memoir on the inscriptions of Kirmanshah), Marc Joseph Müller, Professor at the University of Munich, took a fresh start in his admirable 'Essai sur la langue Pehlvie', published in the 'Journal Asiatique' (April 1839). This is the first paper written to elucidate the Pahlavî of the books in a truly scientific spirit. He started from the Pahlavî alphabet published by Anquetil, and especially from the critical remarks, made by the celebrated Danish scholar, E. Rask, on some of the values ascribed by Anquetil to several Pahlavî characters [2]). Several of his objections he successfully maintained; for instance, he showed, by numerous examples, that the final *k*, which is considered by the Desturs either as an equivalent of *h*, or as a mute, was originally a real *k* and pronounced as such, e. g. *apestâk*, Syr. ܐܦܣܬܐܩ, Arab. ابستاق. His remarks on the value of , which he proves to be *âi* and not *â* (although the character used for *â* in Zand is of the same form), are very sagacious. He also made a successful attempt at elucidating the most difficult part of Pahlavî writing, the homonymity of some letters, that is,

1) 'Commentationes IV de numis veterum Persarum', in Comment. Soc. Reg. Scient. Gott. rec. T. I—IV. 1808—13.

2) See Journal Asiatique for 1823, vol. II. pag. 143—150. The article refers both to the Zand and Pahlavî alphabets, and had been communicated to Sylvestre de Sacy who had it printed.

the fact that several sounds are expressed by one and the same character. He started with the traditional readings of the Pahlavî characters, but did not hestitate to correct them, when they were contradicted by sound etymology; thus, he showed that cannot be read *boman*, as the Parsis pronounce it, but בנמן *benman*, as is evidently identical with the Hebr. בֵּן, Chald. בַּר. Although this essay contains many valuable remarks, and shows the sound scholarship of its author, it is incomplete, as only part of the alphabet has been discussed in it, and the grammar was left untouched.

In the following year (1840), Longpérier published a comprehensive work on the Sasanian coins, entitled 'Essai sur les médailles des rois perses de la dynastie sassanide (Paris)'. It contained the description and figures of a large number of coins struck by the Sasanian rulers, from Ardeshîr I. to Yazdagird III. (or IV.), that is, from the rise to the fall of the Sasanian dynasty (A.D. 226—640). Some names hitherto undeciphered on coins, but readable without difficulty, were read by him for the first time, such as Kobad (*Kavât*); that of Yazdagird had already been hinted at by Tychsen; but some of his readings of names were doubtful, such as Shehryâr and Azermidokht. Excepting names, no fresh addition to our knowledge of Pahlavî, was made by Longpérier, who had scarcely anything to guide him save the readings of De Sacy and Sir W. Ouseley. His work however, as a collection of all the then available material, was a considerable advance in Pahlavî numismatics, and exhibits very clearly the difference, in form, of the Pahlavî characters of the earlier and later centuries of the Sasanian rule. The author justly remarked, that there is but little difference between the characters on the later coins and those used in the MSS.

A decided advance in our knowledge of the inscriptional Pahlavî, was made by J. Olshausen, in his pamphlet on the Pahlavî legends which are found on the coins of the later Sasanian kings, on the earlier coins of the Khalifs, on the coins of the Ispehbeds of Taberistân, and on the Indo-Persian coins of east-Iran (1843) [1]. He may justly lay claim to have deciphered, for the first time, the legends on the classes of coins just mentioned; and he discovered names, numerals written in words, and other terms, which had not been read by any of his predecessors. On a certain class of coins, for instance, he read the name Tapûristân (the country of Taberistân), together with some other proper names and numerals. Some of the coins have only Pahlavî legends, while others have legends both in Pahlavî and Kufic characters; some of the proper names are Arabic, such as ʻOmar and Hârûn, others are Persian, such as Khurshîd. He deciphered the term [illegible] *afzût*, ʻcrescat!ʼ which is of such frequent occurrence on the later Sasanian coins. He also read, on the earlier coins of the Arab governors, the names [illegible] *Khorâsân*, *Omari-Ubeid-allâ-ân*, i. e. ʻOmar the son of Ubeid Allah, etc.ʼ

The decipherment of the legends on Sasanian coins now began to receive more attention from oriental scholars. B. Dorn devoted to the subject, several papers which were published in the ʻBulletin de la classe historico-philologique de l'Académie Impériale des sciences de St. Petersbourgʼ (vol. I. 1844, pag. 107—110, 207—272 and 274—294.) He made no fresh discoveries of any importance, but read the names, which were already known from De Sacy's and Longpérier's works, on all the Pahlavî coins accessible to him. He still retained the erroneous reading כה for [illegible] *bagî*, ʻdivineʼ, which had been proposed by De Sacy. Our knowledge of Pahlavî numismatics has, however, considerably gained by his description of coins which had not been accessible to any other Pahlavî scholar.

A. Krafft published, in 1844, a valuable review [2]) of Olshausen's

---

1) The pamphlet is in German, and its title is: ʻDie Pehlewi-Legenden auf den Münzen der letzten Sasaniden, auf den ältesten Münzen arabischer Chalifen, auf den Münzen der Ispehbeds von Taberistân und auf den indo-persischen Münzen des östlichen Irân, zum erstenmale gelesen und erklärt von Dr. Justus Olshausen. Kopenhagen, 1843ʼ.

2) The German title is: ʻUeber Herrn Professor Olshausen's Entzifferung der Pehlewi-Legenden auf Münzenʼ.

pamphlet, in the 'Wiener Jahrbücher für Literatur' (vol. 106, Anzeige-blatt, pag. 1—33). He gave some information regarding the native rulers of Taberistân and the subsequent Arab governors of the province, and the different dynasties to which they belonged; and especially endeavoured to settle their chronology, by aid of the coins on which numbers referring to an era are found, the commencement of which he placed at A. D. 645. He likewise deciphered the legends on the Pahlavî coins of the Vienna collection.

It appears that the discoveries of Olshausen, whose pamphlet had been translated into English (London Numismatic Chronicle for 1848, vol. IX.) induced E. Thomas, of the Bengal Civil Service, to investigate the Pahlavî coins of the earlier Arab rulers. He published a very comprehensive essay on this subject, in the 'Journal of the Royal Asiatic Society of Great Britain' for 1850 (vol. XII. pag. 253—347.) As the material at his disposal was more extensive than that used by Olshausen, he was able (aided by the latter's discoveries) to make a further advance in the decipherment of the legends on the later Pahlavî coins. He described, *a)* the coins of 'the purely initiative, imitative coinage of the Arabs, from A. H. 18 to 43', during which period the Arab conquerors used the coins of the later Sasanian kings, or struck coins with similar dies, bearing Pahlavî legends, merely with the addition of the words بسم الله; *b)* the coins of the Arab governors, viz. Ziad bin Abu Sofian, Obeidullah bin Ziad, Selim-i Ziad, Abdallah bin Zobeir, Abdallah bin Hazim and others of the first century of the Hijra era, down to Hejaj bin Yusaf (A. H. 81). He also showed that these later coins bore the names of the mint cities, on the right side of their reverse; and he tried to identify some of these names, such as  = بصره *Basrah* and  = يزد *Yezd.* Whether this was an independent discovery of Thomas, or whether it was suggested by the remarks of Mordtmann to the same effect, does not clearly appear; suffice it to say, that Mordtmann's note on the subject appeared in 1848 (Zeitschrift der Deutschen Morgenländischen Gesellschaft, vol. II. pag. 112), whereas Thomas's essay was read in June 1849. He likewise added a valuable note 'regarding the unidentified characters composing the legends on certain classes of Sasanian coins'. Some of these coins which are depicted in Wilson's 'Ariana antiqua', had from their singularity (as they also bear Indian characters), already attracted attention; but the honor of having first more minutely examined them, belongs certainly to Thomas. He treated of these coins more fully, in a separate note to his edition of 'Prinsep's essays on Indian antiquities', 1858 (vol. II. pag. 107—116); and in the same edition, he has made several other scattered remarks on Pahlavî coins (vol. I. pag. 12—15, 32—35, 62—72, 93—96 and 120—126.) He has also published several articles, on the same subjects, in the 'London Numismatic Chronicle', which is however not accessible to me.

In all his writings, Thomas shows himself to be a skilful palæographer, who can identify characters which are difficult to read; but in his philological explanations he is not very successful.

Let us now return to the Pahlavî of the books. After the publication of M. Jos. Müller's essay on the Pahlavî language, which has been already noticed, nothing appeared on this subject, for about twelve years (from want of easily accessible materials), except a very valuable essay by the same author, containing researches into the opening chapter of the Bundehesh (1843). [1]) It was written with a view to settle the position (in Zoroastrian theology) of *zarvan akarana*, 'time without bounds', which is mentioned in the Bundehesh.

In 1851, N. L. Westergaard published a lithographed facsimile [2]) of the oldest codex of the Bundehesh (written A. D. 1330) which had

1) Its German title is: 'Untersuchungen über den Anfang des Bundehesch', published in the Abhandlungen der ersten Classe der K. bayerischen Akademie der Wissenschaften, vol. III. pag. 615—644. A separate impression of it has also been published.

2) Bundehesh, liber Pehlvicus. E vetustissimo codice Havniensi descripsit, duas inscriptiones regis Saporis primi adjecit N. L. Westergaard, professor Havniensis. Havniæ. Impensis Librariæ Gyldendalianæ lapidibus excudebant Bing et Ferslew. 1851.

been brought from India by Rask, and is now preserved in the library at Copenhagen. He added two Sasanian inscriptions, each in a different kind of Pahlavî character, which he had copied himself at Hâjîâbâd, when travelling in Persia; and in the preface, he hinted that the language of these inscriptions differs very considerably from the Pahlavî of the books.

In 1853, another and more important text, viz. the Pahlavî translation of the Vendidâd, was published by Fr. Spiegel, who had been enabled, by the liberality of the Bavarian goverment, to copy the most valuable Zand and Pahlavî MSS. which are extant in the libraries at Paris, Copenhagen, London (British Museum and India Office) and Oxford, the only places in Europe where such MSS. are to be found [1]). And in 1858, it was followed by the Pahlavî (Huzvâresh) texts of the Yasna and Vîsparad [2]).

Shortly after the publication of the Huzvâresh text of the Vendidâd, the writer of this essay began the study of Pahlavî, with no other materials but those furnished by that text and that of the Bundehesh, together with Anquetil's Pahlavî-Pâzand vocabulary and his translation of the Bundehesh. The results were published in the form of a review of Westergard's Bundehesh, which appeared in the 'Göttinger Gelehrte Anzeigen' of 1854 [3]). In this review, the present writer made the *first* attempt at giving a short sketch of Pahlavî grammar (pag. 7—22); to which he

---

1) A sixth collection, which is particularly rich in Pahlavî MSS., is in my own possession.

2) Avesta. Die heiligen Schriften der Parsen. Zum ersten Male im Grundtext sammt der Huzvâresh-Uebersetzung herausgegeben von Friedrich Spiegel. Vol. I. Vendidâd. Vienna, 1853. Vol. II. Vîsparad and Yasna. Vienna, 1858.

As this edition of the Pahlavî texts was prepared from insufficient material, I recommended the Bombay goverment to employ Destur Hoshengjî in the preparation of a more correct edition, with glossaries of all the words which occur; the MS. of the Pahlavî text of the Vendidâd is now ready, and its glossary is being prepared.

3) A separate impression of it was published under the title: 'Ueber die Pehlewi-Sprache und den Bundehesh, von Martin Haug. Göttingen 1854', (in der Dieterich'schen Buchandlung.)

added a translation of the first three chapters of the Bundehesh. He also endeavoured to decipher some words of the two Sapor inscriptions at Hâjîâbâd which, except the titles, had not been previously read by any scholar; he made this attempt, in order to form an opinion as to the relationship between the inscriptional Pahlavî and that of the books, and he came to the conclusion that there was, in the main, little difference between the two inscriptional languages and that of the books, as all three exhibit the same character, viz. a mixture of Semitic and Iranian elements. With respect to the Semitic words, he believed them to belong to some eastern Aramaic dialect, standing nearest to the Chaldee, but not identical with it; and as regards the general character of the language, he declared it to be Iranian. His pamphlet, on the whole, contained the first detailed investigation into the character of the language.

I may here call attention to some valuable remarks made, in 1854, by Westergaard on Pahlavî, in the preface to his edition of the Zend-avesta (pag. 19—21). He distinguished between the *Sasanian Pahlavî* found in inscriptions, and the *Zand-Pahlavî* of the books; the first he considered as a Semitic tongue, intermixed with Persian words; and the second as a purely Iranian language, identical with the *Pâzand*, or older form of the modern Persian; the Semitic words in the latter being, in his opinion, only arbitrary or ideographic signs.

Whilst these attempts were made to investigate the language of the Pahlavî books, the legends on coins were by no means neglected. In 1854, Dr. Mordtmann, of Constantinople, published a most comprehensive and valuable essay on the coins with Pahlavî legends [1]). He divided them into four classes: *a*) Sasanian coins (A. D. 226—651); *b*) the older Mohamedan pieces coined by the Arab governors (down to A. D. 700), with legends in Pahlavi and Kufic characters; *c*) coins of the rulers of

1) 'Erklärung der Münzen mit Pehlevi-Legenden, von Dr. A. D. Mordtmann', in the 'Zeitschrift der Deutschen Morgenländischen Gesellschaft', (vol. VIII. pag. 1—194.)

Taberistân (down to A. D. 800); *d)* coins of the eastern provinces of Persia, which exhibit Devanâgarî and other characters which are unintelligible, besides the Pahlavî. The material at his disposal was the most extensive that had been available to any scholar; for he states that he had been able to examine about 2000 Pahlavî coins, ranging from the time of Ardeshîr Bâbegân, down to the latest coins with Pahlavî legends, struck under the Arab rule. His researches extended however, only to the first three classes of coins; the fourth, or so-called Indo-Sasanian, class, which is the most difficult to handle, he does not appear to have examined.

The legends on the coins are divided by him into eight classes, which follow one another almost in chronological order. Here we need only observe, that at first, the name of the king with all his titles appeared on the obverse, while on the reverse the name was repeated with the addition of some other word [1]); this repetition alone enabled De Sacy to decipher the legends on the earlier Sasanian coins, as the same names and titles appear in about the same form; in the course of time (from Behrâm IV., A. D. 389—399) the titles were shortened, and frequently only *malkân malkâ*, 'king of kings', was used; on those of Hormazd III. (A. D. 457—458) and Piruz (A. D. 458—485) even this title was omitted, and merely the name was given, with some benedictive formula, such as *afzût*, and this custom was continued till the end of the Sasanian rule.

---

1) As a specimen, I give here the legends on a coin of Ardeshîr:

Round the obverse.

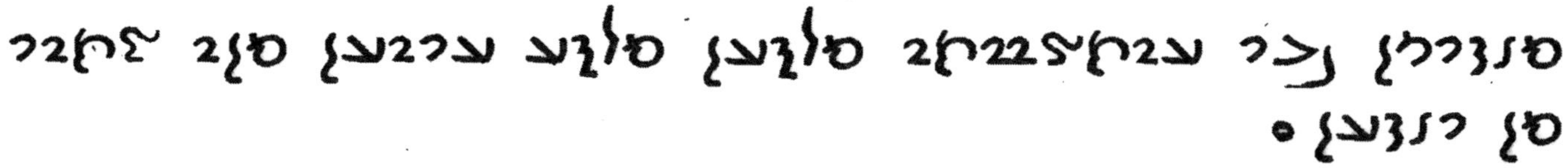

Mazdayasn bagî Artakhshatr malkân malkâ Aîrân minû chitrî min yazdân.

'The Mazdâ-worshipping divine Artakhshatr, king of the kings of Irân, of spiritual origin from God'.

On the reverse.

Left side.

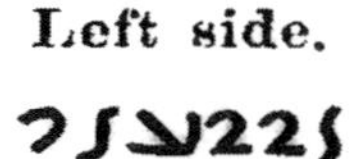

Nûvâzî.

Right side.

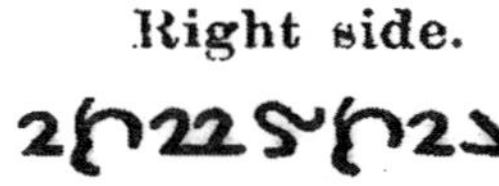

Artakhshatr.

From a palæographic point of view, that is, as regards the shapes of the Pahlavî characters, he divided the coins into three periods: *a*) those whose alphabet is identical with that used in the rock inscriptions, (from Ardeshîr to Nersi, A. D. 226—300); *b*) those whose letters are intermediate in form, between the lapidary alphabet and that of the books (A. D. 300—600); *c*) those whose alphabet is identical with that of the books (A. D. 600 — 800).

Notwithstanding the extent of his material, Mordtmann did not rest satisfied with his researches, but deeply interested in the subject, he sought for more, and examined 3000 more coins, in addition to the 2000 previously mentioned. His further researches, the aim of which was to complete and rectify his former ones, were published in two subsequent articles, in the Journal of the German Oriental Society for 1858 and 1865 [1]). He also wrote an essay, in which he explained the Pahlavî inscriptions on seals [2]).

His results, so far as they went beyond those obtained by De Sacy and Olshausen, were contested, especially by B. Dorn [3]), Bartholomæi [4]) and Khanykov [5]), who seem to represent the Russian branch of Pahlavî numismatists. They specially objected to his explaining certain words and abbreviations, on the reverse of the later coins, as the names of the mint cities; also to his treatment of the Kobad and Khosru coins, etc. But although the observations of Dorn contain much valuable matter, and even some real corrections of Mordtmann's readings, the latter appears to be right as regards the mint cities. His opponents are undecided how to

1) Zeitschrift der Deutschen Morgenländischen Gesellschaft, vol. XII. pag. 1 — 56, XIX. pag. 373 — 496.

2) Studien über geschnittene Steine mit Pehlevi Inschriften; Zeitschr. d. D M. G. vol. XVIII, of 1864, pag. 1 — 47.

3) Mélanges asiatiques, St. Petersburg, vol. III, of 1858—59, pag. 149—165, 426—459, 460—475 and 502—531.

4) Mélanges asiatiques, vol. III, pag. 139 — 165 and 349 — 372. And Bulletin historico-philologique, vol. XIV. pag. 371—378.

5) In a letter addressed to B. Dorn.

read the words and signs which he so interprets; they suppose they may be the names of the die-cutters, or signs indicating the value of the coin, or honorific epithets; but all these opinions seem groundless, and have been very ably refuted by Mordtmann [1]), and I doubt if they will ever find favor with oriental scholars out of Russia.

Notwithstanding the objections which may be raised against his treatment of Pahlavî numismatics, no impartial scholar can deny that Mordtmann has greatly advanced our knowledge of this branch of antiquarian research. His judgment is sound, his oriental scholarship and acquaintance with the Byzantine, Arab, Persian and Armenian historians (who are the chief sources of information regarding the Sasanian kings), is very considerable, and his zeal is indefatigable; so we may hope for further contributions from him [2]), for the advance of our knowledge in Pahlavî numismatics and the history of the Sasanian kings.

Two years after the publication of my short sketch of Pahlavî grammar, Spiegel gave to the world his 'Huzvâresh grammar' [3]), which treated of the same subject, on a much more extensive scale. His attention was principally directed to the Pahlavi of the books; that which is found on coins and in inscriptions was treated by him in an appendix, in which he merely registered the results obtained by De Sacy, Olshausen, Mordtmann, etc., without making any researches of his own.

The works which he used for preparing his grammar of the Pahlavi of the books, were the Pahlavî translations of the Vendidâd, Yasna and Visparad, with the Bundehesh, which are a mere fraction of the whole Pahlavi literature, and do not afford any great variety of style; moreover, these texts had never been critically examined, and many of their readings are either doubtful, or erroneous. If we take into account this insufficiency

1) In an article in the Zeitschrift der D. M. G. vol. XIX. pag. 373—413.

2) His latest contribution is: 'Hecatompylos' (the capital city of the Arsacidæ), in the 'Sitzungsberichte der K. bayerischen Akademie der Wissenschaften, 1869', pag. 497—536.

3) Grammatik der Huzvâresh-Sprache, von Fr. Spiegel. Wien, 1856; 194 pages.

of material and the great difficulty of the subject, both as regards the written characters and the language, we cannot expect from him anything very complete, or accurate. It must, however, be acknowledged that he has registered a good many grammatical facts, and his work is useful as a collection of materials, for those who intend making researches of their own into the Pahlavî language.

As regards his views on the character of the language, and his explanations of its non-Iranian element, linguists are not likely to feel satisfied; for instance, no scholar of sound judgment can place the slightest confidence in his opinion regarding the origin of the personal pronouns, which form, according to him, a very curious medley drawn from various languages; thus, he derives 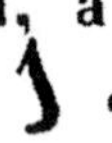 'I', from the Afghanic [1]), 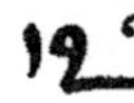 'his, it', from the Kurdish, and  'we', from the Semitic languages. Such a proceeding would no doubt be ridiculed, if applied to some better known language; for instance, if any one now-a-days were to derive the pronoun 'I' from Russian, 'we' from French, and 'he' from Celtic, the general verdict upon his opinions can well be imagined.

Spiegel is equally unfortunate in his explanation of those verbal forms which end in 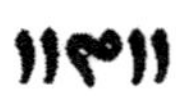 and 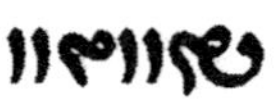 (traditionally read *ôntan* and *îtôntan*), and are all evidently of Semitic origin. For instance, he reads *dehavanntann* for  'to be' (traditionally *jânôntan*), although he accepts the derivation from Chald. הֲוָא 'to be', which I had already proposed in my sketch of Pahlavî grammar mentioned above. The initial  of the Semitic verbs, he reads *d* in all cases where the Desturs read it *j*, without however giving any explanation of this prefix, but merely comparing it with the Armenian prefix *z* (e. g. *zantzanēl* = *antzanēl* 'to transgress'), in which I can see nothing but the remnant of a preposition; but of what preposition is  a relic? or is it at all likely that a Semitic

1) This language cannot even be included among the proper Iranian tongues; it is much more akin to the Indian vernaculars than to the Persian dialects, as has been shown beyond doubt by Dr. Trumpp, in two valuable papers on this language, which appeared in the Journal of the German Oriental Society, vol. XXI and XXII.

verb would be compounded with an inseparable Aryan prefix, in much the same way as one might compound an English verb with the Arabic prefix سَ, by writing *sa-be, sa-is* for 'will be'? Again, he takes *ann* as an Aryan participial termination *an*, but for the second *n* he does not account. The final *tann* is of course the Persian termination of the infinitive, but this does not explain the second *n*, for in what Aryan language do the infinitives end in *nn?* If Spiegel's views were correct, the word [illegible] would, therefore, consist: *a*) of an unusual Aryan prefix, *b*) of a Semitic root, and *c*) of two modified Aryan suffixes; and the infinitive would be formed from the present participle, but can this be shown to be the case in any Iranian tongue? for instance, can the Persian *guftan* 'to speak' be traced to a participle?

On a careful consideration of these arguments, probably no sound scholar would be satisfied to adhere to Spiegel's reading of [illegible], but we have besides a positive proof that it is wrong, by the freqnent occurrence of the word in the Sasanian inscriptions, where it is written [illegible] which can only be read *yahvûn*, or *yahvôn*, as [illegible] has no other phonetical value than *î*, or *y*, (see the index, pag. 234). In other cases also, where Spiegel reads *d* for [illegible], the inscriptions use [illegible] *y*, as in [illegible] *yekavîmûnt* = [illegible] (see pag. 255), and [illegible] *yaktîbûn* = [illegible] (see inscription of Naksh-i Rajab, lin. 25). These instances, with others, also show that [illegible] must be read *ûn*, or *ôn*, when found following Semitic roots in crude verbal forms, as its equivalent in the Sasanian inscriptions is [illegible] *ûn*, *ôn*, which cannot be read *nn* [1]); the traditional reading *ûn*, *ôn*, of [illegible] by the Desturs, is therefore confirmed by the inscriptions.

Spiegel's reading *anman*, *hanman*, for the auxiliary verb [illegible], is

1) The only instance which seems exceptional, is in Westergaard's copy of the Hâjîâbâd inscription A. (Bund. pag. 83). where in lin. 6 we read [illegible] *shadîtann*, but according to Stannus's plaster cast of the inscription, there is no second *n*, neither is there one, in the same word, in lin. 5 of Westergaard's copy.

also refuted by the inscriptions, in which it often occurs and is always written *hûman*, which cannot be read *hanman* (see pag. 128).

He has likewise been unfortunate in his explanations of the dative particle, the pronoun, and the particle (see pag. 226, 227, 222—223). As regards the nature of the Pahlavî language, which he calls **Huzvâresh** without sufficient reason (as we shall hereafter see), he considers it an Iranian tongue with an intermixture of Semitic words; but this opinion, which I also shared, we shall find reason to consider incorrect. The Semitic portion he traces to the Nabathæan language, and believes the Huzvâresh to have originated in Sevad, i. e. Chaldæa, in the second century of our era; opinions which prove untenable on further researches.

Although I cannot agree with many of his explanations, nor with his general views of Pahlavî grammar, I readily acknowledge that he has done good service, by collecting many (often too many) examples, and by giving now and then correct explanations. I reviewed the work in detail in 1857, in the Göttinger Gelehrte Anzeigen (Stücke 68—71), to which paper I may refer the reader. A Pahlavî grammar is still a desideratum, and the want has been felt by many, especially by the decipherers of inscriptional Pahlavî, who do not seem to place much confidence in Spiegel's researches.

In 1860, Spiegel published, as a second part to his grammar, a work on the traditional literature of the Parsis, with original texts, translations and a glossary [1]). It contains very valuable notices of various Pahlavî works for those European scholars who have no access to a Pahlavî library. He treats of the Pahlavî translations of some parts of the Avesta, viz. the Vendidâd, Yasna and Visparad, and discusses the method followed by the translators, and the value of their renderings and the glosses which they frequently intermix. He endeavours to show that the Christian

---

1) Die traditionelle Literatur der Parsen, in ihrem Zusammenhange mit den angränzenden Literaturen dargestellt, von Fr. Spiegel. Wien, 1860.

literature of the Syrian church had some influence, not only upon the ideas and the divine worship of the Zoroastrians, but even upon the external appearance of the Pahlavî books, such as their size, their division into chapters and verses, and the colophons in which the writers state the day, month and year, in which they finished their transcript; but his arguments have no more value than his supposition that Zoroaster conversed with Abraham, and borrowed his ideas from him; as similar divisions and colophons occur in Indian MSS. His critical remarks on the Pahlavî translations are also far from satisfactory, and a new and more searching investigation of this important subject, is wanted. The question of their age he does not discuss, nor does he enumerate all the Pahlavî translations which are extant.

After his remarks on the Pahlavî translations, he goes on to enumerate the works of the later literature of the Parsis, so far as they are known to him, which are partly Huzvâresh, and partly Pârsî and Persian. He treats successively of the Bundehesh, of which he states the general contents, translates some chapters [1]), and gives some extracts; of the Ardâi Virâf-nâmeh, according to Pope's English translation; of the Bahman yasht, according to the Pahlavî text in one of Anquetil's MSS.; of the Mînokhirad, some passages of which he translates; of the Rivâyats; of the Sad-der Bundehesh, according to a Persian version; and then follow scanty notices of some smaller works in Persian, such as the Zertosht-nâmeh, Jâmâsp-nâmeh, Shâyist-nishâyist, etc.; the interesting Shikan-gumânî is barely mentioned; with its contents the author seems to be wholly unacquainted. There are a good many appendices, containing transliterations of the Pahlavî texts, in Hebrew characters, of the 1st, 2d, 3d and 31st chapters of the Bundehesh, and the 5th and 19th fargards of the Vendidâd; also texts in the original characters, such as Destur Dârâb's version of the 5th fargard and a Patet,

---

1) The first chapter had been already transliterated in Hebrew characters, translated and explained by him in 1857 in the Zeitschrift der D. Morgenl. Ges. vol. XI, pag. 98—110.

and some extracts from the Rivâyats referring to some of the heroes of the Shâhnâmeh. At the end is a glossary of the Pahlavî words, in Hebrew and Pahlavî characters, for which the author deserves great credit, as it is the first attempt to prepare a Pahlavî glossary in the European fashion; but, as might be expected in a first attempt, the results are not much to be relied on, especially as regards the explanation of the Semitic words.

The author believes he has given his readers a view of the whole range of Pahlavî literature 1), but in this he is mistaken, for not even a fifth part of the still existing Pahlavî literature was then known to him. For instance, he had no knowledge of the largest and most important work of all, the Dîn-kart, which would alone comprise 2000 folio pages, if printed; nor of the Dâdestân-i-dîni, which is nearly thrice as large as the Bundehesh; nor of the Neringistân, which is one-third larger than the Bundehesh; nor of several minor works, such as the Kâr-nâmeh-i Ardeshîr Bâbegân, the Pandnâmehs of Adarbât Mahraspand 2) and Buzurji Mihir, etc., which are all well-known to Pahlavî scholars in India.

The title of this work, 'the traditional literature of the Parsis, in its connection with the conterminous literatures', is therefore more pretentious than appropriate, and calculated to mislead superficial readers, as he was acquainted with only a small fraction of the 'traditional literature', and of the 'conterminous literatures', by which he appears to mean chiefly the Syriac, his knowledge seems to be even less than that of Pahlavî, if we may judge from what appears in this work. His translations even from Persian can only be used with caution, as Destur Hoshengji, who is a

---

1) In the preface to his Huzvâresh grammar (pag. X.), he actually claims to have read and understood the largest portion of Huzvâresh literature. No Parsi priest would assent to this statement, but would think it rather presumptuous, as the study of the whole existing Pahlavî literature might well occupy a lifetime.

2) This has been lately published, with several transliterations, a Gujarâtî translation, notes and a Pahlavî-Gujarâtî-English vocabulary, by Herbad Shehriarji Dadabhoy, at Bombay, 1869, as a Haug's prize essay; the author having obtained the prize proposed by me, for such a work, in 1864.

better Pahlavî and Persian scholar than Spiegel, frequently showed me. A proper title for the work would be: 'Contributions towards a knowledge of the traditional literature of the Parsis, with occasional hints on its probable connection with the literature of the Syrian church, with appendices aud a glossary' [1]).

I may here mention Windischmann's German translation of the Bundehesh, with notes [2]), which was published by Spiegel (1863), after the author's premature death. That European scholars have paid more attention to the Bundehesh than to other Pahlavî works, may surprise my Parsi readers, who do not generally attach much value to this work; but this is easily accounted for by its contents (see pag. 3), in which European scholars take a great interest, and from the circumstance that it had already been made somewhat familiar in Europe by Anquetil's translation, and Westergaard's publication of a facsimile of the old Copenhagen codex of it. In his translation, Windischmann could only use this text and Anquetil's work; if therefore we take into consideration the scantiness of his means, and their insufficiency for arriving at a complete understanding of the numerous particulars and rare words occurring in the Bundehesh, we may well admire the translator for what he has achieved.

Although the text of the Bundehesh, as well as a tolerable translation were before the public, an edition based upon all available materials was still a desideratum. A young and industrious scholar, F. Justi of Marburg, who had already made himself known by the rather premature publication of a so-called 'Old-Bactrian (Zand) Dictionary' [3]), came forward

---

1) On this occasion I may mention an intersting article by Dr. Sachau which is published in the Journal of the Royal Asiatic Society (New Series vol. IV, 1.). It bears the modest title of 'Contributions to the knowledge of Parsee literature', but contains much information which will be sought for in vain in Spiegel's far more pretentious work.

2) In the 'Zoroastrische Studien', pag. 56—120. There is besides, in this work, a separate chapter on the geography of the Bundehesh (pag. 1—19.)

3) I have already shown on several occasions, and finally in my German pamphlet 'on the present state of Zand philology, with special reference to F. Justi's

to supply the want. He published, in 1868, an edition with the Pahlavî text lithographed, a transliteration into Persian characters, a German translation, various readings and a glossary. On the title-page (Der Bundehesh

---

so-called Old-Bactrian Dictionary (Stuttgart, 1868)', that this work is very unsatisfactory and cannot be regarded as a Zand dictionary, as the author, when he made his compilation, had no such knowledge, either of the original Zand text, or of the Pahlavî translation, as would qualify him to undertake so arduous a task. My pamphlet has not been ineffectual, so far as I can judge from the numerous letters I have received from oriental scholars on the subject. How necessary it was to put all those oriental scholars on their guard, who had not made Zand a special subject of study for a number of years, and were therefore not prepared to detect the shortcomings of the 'Dictionary', may be shown by the circumstance that even so eminent an orientalist as Max Müller has been led astray by it. In the first volume of his 'Rigveda-Sanhita translated and explained' (pag. 206), the celebrated Oxford scholar quotes the explanation of *zairimyañura* in Justi's dictionary, as a proof that the Vedic word *harmya*, which is phonetically identical with the Zand *zairimya*, means originally 'fire-pit', and not only 'house' as the Hindu scholars interpret it; but he has not enquired into the authority for this explanation. Justi interprets *zairimyañura* by 'eating in the depth', but this interpretation, like most of his other explanations, is merely copied from Spiegel, as Müller will find on reference to Spiegel's translation of the Avesta (vol. I. pag. 190—191, note 3.), and the authority for the explanation will be rather unexpected, as Spiegel is entirely guided by Roth's interpretation of this very word *harmya*, as 'depth', in fixing the meaning of *zairimya*, which Müller has quoted as a collateral proof of the meaning of *harmya*, which is decidedly a case of reasoning in a circle. The meaning 'pit, depth', for *harmya*, if strictly investigated, can scarcely be proved from the Vedas, as there is not a single passage, among those quoted, that necessarily requires this meaning, which will probably prove ultimately to be nothing but one of the many guesses of Prof. Roth that young Vedic students must discard, if they wish really to understand the Vedic hymns. *Zairimyañura* itself is interpreted by the Parsi priests as a 'tortoise' (comp. Sans. *harmmuṭa*); the meaning 'eating in the depth', besides being very vague, as it might be applied to a mouse, or a mole, or a hamster, is also in itself too absurd to have ever become the name of an animal.

Professor H. Kern of Leyden has also been misled by Justi and Spiegel. In a recent article on the Persian cuneiform inscriptions, published in the Journal of the German Oriental Society, vol. XXII., he relies (pag. 219) upon Justi's dictionary for the meaning 'protection' for the Zand *yaona*, and tries to restore and explain the cuneiform text in accordance with that meaning. But how far his reliance has been misplaced, Dr. Kern, as a scholar of sense and sound reasoning,

zum ersten Male herausgegeben, übersetzt und mit Glossar versehen von Ferdinand Justi) he claims to have published all this for the first time, which is only strictly correct as regards the glossary. The honor

---

will readily see on examining the pasages in which the word occurs. Let us take the passage Yt. 5, 87. *thwãm kaininô vadhrê yaona khshathra hvâhâo jaidhyâoñti,* which is thus translated by Justi: 'the marriageable girls pray thee in a sisterly way for a rule which wards off (i. e. a husband, a lord)'. Now in the first place, can any man of sound logic suppose that young girls could have addressed a prayer, couched in such odd terms, to the deity Anâhitâ, if they prayed for a husband? Besides, the following words *takhmemcha nmânô-paitîm* 'a strong husband', forbid such an interpretation, as the idea of 'husband' would thus be expressed twice, first by *yaona khshathra,* which is Justi's 'rule which wards off', and secondly by the appropriate words. On a closer examination, it will be found that Justi has completely misunderstood three words in the sentence, viz. *vadhrê, yaona* and *hvâhâo.* To the first he ascribes the meaning 'marriageable', which he has simply copied from Spiegel; no other proof is adduced but the supposed etymology from *vad* 'to marry', and no attempt is made to connect it with *vadhairi* which is evidently the same, but to which the meaning 'belonging to a caravan' is ascribed, without any proof, but tracing it to the same root *vad* in the sense 'to go', which it never has in Zand. It would be much more natural to identify *vadhrê* with the Vedic *vadhri* (Rv. 1, 32, 7. 33, 6. 2, 25, 3. etc.) which means 'a male deprived of his sexual powers, an eunuch'; *vadhairi* is generally applied to the camel, in which case it can only mean 'gelded'. *Yaona* is taken by Justi in the sense of 'warding off', but of course no proof is given save an etymology tracing it to *yu* 'to join' (the root *yu* 'to ward off' seems to have been forgotten). But besides this meaning of 'warding off', he ascribes three others to *yaona,* viz. *a)* connection, residence; *b)* the airy region; *c)* power; but all these will be found by Dr. Kern, on closer enquiry, just as fanciful as that of 'warding off'; for none of the passages quoted can be really explained by any of them. Thus Justi (following Spiegel) translates Vend. 21, 6. *hãmyaċtâoñhô yaonemcha avi zãmcha, zãmcha avi yaonemcha,* by 'it draws the air to the earth, and the earth to the air' but I doubt whether this would be considered intelligible by either Müller or Kern. In the whole explanation of *yaona,* there is, I think, only one statement which is correct; for at the end, he compares it with the Sans. *yoni,* which is no doubt identical with *yaona,* but has none of the meanings assigned to the latter by the writer, except perhaps 'residence' which seems merely accessory in his opinion; *yoni* means 'womb' and also 'home, place, house, space', and these meanings alone are applicable to *yaona* in all passages. — Thus, Vend. 21, 6. is to be translated: 'they (the waters) are striving for their home (to reach it) and the earth, for the earth and for their home' (that is to say, they issue from their home, which is the lake *Vourukasha,* and

of having published the Pahlavî text 'for the first time' belongs to Westergaard; (his edition is a facsimile of a MS. at Copenhagen, that is the oldest known to exist, having been written in A. D. 1330; next in age is one in my possession, written in A. D. 1396, but belonging to a different class of MSS., commencing with the 15th chapter, like the MS. 121 in the Ouseley collection of the Bodleian library, but more complete.) For the transliteration, which is in the Persian character, Justi had the assistance of a Pâzand Bundehesh, where the Pahlavî words are written

---

are poured on the earth, and after having been poured on the earth, they return to their home again). Again Vend. 4, 45., *ukhshnê khrathwê yaonê âstê* means clearly, 'he (the student) sits at home to improve his knowledge'; but Justi's translation is, 'that he may remain in connection (with purity joined through prayer) for the growth of the intellect'; vague and scarcely intelligible statements of this kind are quite foreign to the Vendidâd. — How is the meaning 'protection' to be proved? Dr. Kern* thinks it follows of necessity from such compounds as *perethuyaona*, *huyaona* and *hvâyaona;* but on examining the passages he will find rather strange ideas result from the application of this meaning; for instance, *hvâyaona* is an epithet of *garô-demâna* 'paradise'; how can this be termed 'protected by itself'? such an idea is quite foreign to Zoroastrianism; but the true meaning is 'having its own place, its own abode' i. e. being on a separate spot, not assigned to anything else; so also *perethuyaona* means 'having a wide place, home or abode'. Returning now to Yt. 5, 87. the third word misunderstood in it, is *hvâhâo;* this is made to mean 'sisterly, like a sister'; but without taking into consideration the etymological difficulty of deriving *hvâhâo* from *qanhar* 'sister', it can scarcely be supposed that young girls would regard a goddess as a sister; nor could it mean 'like a sister', even if the derivation were correct, for *hvâhâo* must be either a substantive or adjective, governed either by *jaidhyâoñti* or by *khshathra*, but cannot be an adverb. As the word occurs only in this place, its exact meaning can be scarcely ascertained. I propose translating the whole of clause 87 thus: 'girls whose womb is barren pray thee for the possession of fertility (?) and for a strong husband; young women who are pregnant pray thee for a good delivery; thou who possessest this, wilt bestow that upon them, O Ardvî sûra Anâhitâ'.

Want of space alone prevents me from discussing other instances, in which Dr. Kern has been misled by Justi's copying Spiegel; but the above remarks may be sufficient to convince both Dr. Kern and M. Müller, that the 'Old-Bactrian Dictionary' can be used only with great caution, as they can further see from my pamphlet mentioned above, for articles like that on *yaona*, in which nearly all the explanation is incorrect, are not unfrequent in that book.

in the easily legible Zand characters; it cannot therefore be considered a first attempt. He differs, of course, very frequently from the traditional readings, and not always with advantage, as he is a faithful copyist of Spiegel, even of his gravest errors, such as *nad* for *vad* ود, *ajash* for *avash* or *apash* ایوس (as the Sasanian inscriptions show beyond doubt), *dehavûntann* (where *ûn* is certainly an improvement upon Spiegel's *nn*) for *yehavûntanu* ںوںرسوں, etc. (see pag. 16. 17), and as these are all words of frequent occurrence, every page is full of errors that must be very perplexing to the Pahlavî student.

In the translation he has relied chiefly on Windischmann's translation, improving it mostly in those places where he found more correct readings in the additional MSS. he used; it is not very readable, and in some places almost as unintelligible as Spiegel's translation of the Vendidâd. Any reader of it, who has any acquaintance with Pahlavî, will do well to refer to the original text, as has been already pointed out by Dr. E. Sachau (now Professor at Vienna) in his able review of the work (Zeitschrift der D. Morg. Ges. vol XXII. pag. 506.) The very commencement of the chapter, with which Justi's edition begins, he appears to have misunderstood. That chapter commences with a heading, as I have already shown in my pamphlet 'Ueber die Pehlewi Sprache und den Bundehesh'; the words سوںدں کرد ک *men zand âkâs* 'from the *Zand-âkâs*' (one who knows the Zand, Zand teacher), denote the source whence the compiler took his statements; for *Zand-âkâs* was evidently the name of some ancient Pahlavî work, now lost. The passage can be simply translated thus: 'From the *Zand-âkâs;* firstly, on the creations of Hormazd and the counter-creations of Aharman; secondly, on the quality of the creatures from the beginning to the end which is the future body (the resurrection)'; that is to say, the compiler of the fragments in question (chap. I—XIV, XXIV—XXVII and XXXI, which follow one another in my old MS.) borrowed all his statements, on the subjects mentioned, from that work. Quotations of this kind are frequently introduced in this way, in Parsi literature, by such words, for instance, as از روایت کامه بهره 'from the Rivâyat of Kâmah Bahrah'.

The most valuable part of the work is, no doubt, the glossary, which is arranged according to the Persian alphabet, the Pahlavi words being given in the Persian character and generally according to Spiegel's readings. This transliteration is a great draw-back, as in a glossary, the original characters are essentially necessary, since the mode of reading many of the compound characters is still very unsettled, and many of Spiegel's readings can be shown to be erroneous, as the reader will see from my remarks above and the index to this volume. Justi has proved himself to be a good index maker, as his glossary is complete, even beyond reasonable bounds, for he quotes all passages in which the 'idhâfat' occurs, and under each word he repeats in most cases all the sentences in which it is found, whereas a simple quotation of page and line would have been quite sufficient. Besides the words found in the Bundehesh, he has inserted those of the Pahlavî-Pâzand glossary, according to one of Anquetil's MSS. which, however, is differently arranged from the text published here.

With regard to the explanations he gives of Pahlavî words, he depends almost entirely on Spiegel's statements, which are generally blindly adopted by him, (thus, he derives the pronoun  'I' from the Afghanic *râ*; for a refutation of which opinion, see the index s. v. *ra*, pag. 189—190). He has therefore not sensibly advanced our knowledge of Pahlavî beyond the point arrived at by Spiegel who, as we have seen, has left it in a very confused state. His collections of information regarding the proper names of various kinds, form the most useful part of his glossary. In tracing Huzvâresh words to their Semitic equivalents, he is particularly unfortunate, especially in those cases where he had not Spiegel's ideas to guide him. Dr. Sachau, in his review (pag. 508—510) above mentioned, has already pointed out several instances which clearly show that Justi's references to Semitic dictionaries have not been quite sufficient for a successful explanation of the more difficult Huzvâresh words, which had not been explained by previous investigators. Thus he traces  'the back' to Chald. אף 'face', 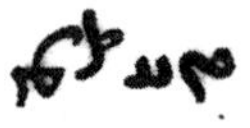 'nose' to Chald. חל 'hill',  'servant' to Chald לפום 'to the mouth', etc.; derivations which seem childish, and

I could fill pages by enumerating and refuting similar absurdities to be found in his glossary, but I have only space to notice his remarks upon Destur Hoshengji's reading  'word' in the traditional way *modâ*, instead of *mandâ* which is Spiegel's reading. The Destur was fully aware of the latter reading, but he was also aware that Spiegel can show no more appropriate meaning for his *mandâ* than 'knowledge', which is a different idea from 'word', he therefore rejected the proposed alteration, and adhered to the traditional reading, till a more satisfactory etymology should be offered; this the reader will find in the index, pag. 159—160, where the word is read *mũnyâ* = *malyâ*, 'word'.

In his introduction, Justi discusses the age of the Bundehesh, the composition of which he places in the time of Firdûsî (A. D. 1000), or even later; for he is not disinclined to believe that the Copenhagen codex (dated A. D. 1330) may have been copied from the original; but none of his proofs are in any way convincing, whether based upon the historical, or geographical, remarks found in the work, or upon philological grounds. It is true the Arab rule is mentioned twice; 57, 3. and 82, 2. (chap. 34); but in both cases in a remark, at the end of a chapter, where it may very probably have been added by later copyists, especially as it tends to complete the short sketch of the history of Iran, contained in ch. 34., which does not properly belong to the Bundehesh, The geographical arguments for a late date, are exceedingly doubtful, since the geography of the Bundehesh is more mythical than real, as any one will soon find on examining the book. The supposed identity of *Kãnsiyâ* with the *Hâmûn* lake in Sejestân has to be proved; for *Kãnsiyâ* is apparently the mythical water *Kãsaoya* of the Zend-avesta, whence the prophets of the world's latest period are expected to rise. The philological proofs appear to be founded upon a grave error, for Justi seems determined to find Arabic words in the Bundehesh; the groundlessness of this assumption has been clearly shown by Dr. Sachau in his review (pag. 503—505) mentioned above; but the derivation of the word 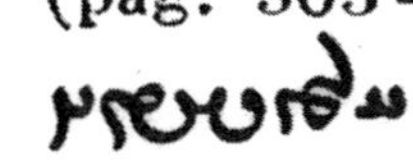 *armôshtîn*, B. 74, 10., (the name of a certain fire) from the Arabic آلْمُشْتَعَل 'inflamed' is particularly absurd, as it can scarcely be supposed that so vague a term as 'inflamed', with a foreign article prefixed, would be borrowed from another language, and made the name of a particular kind of fire; in fact, there is not a single word in the whole Bundehesh that can be proved to belong to the Arabic language exclusively.

If the work had been really composed at so late a date as Justi asserts, we should certainly know the name of the author, but none such is either mentioned, or known. It is merely a collection of detached fragments which have been put together in various ways (as the MSS. show three different modes of arrangement), sometimes with additions, and sometimes with omissions. The statements made in it, are based upon a certain interpretation (a *zand*) of the Avesta, which is always mentioned as the source of the information, and is called *dîn*. As the Bundehesh contains may things which are not found in the present Avesta texts, we must conclude that the author, or authors, had a much larger portion of the Nosks to refer to, than is now extant; and this all points to Sasanian times. The style is very like that of the Naksh-i-Rajab inscription, which is of the end of the 3[d] century A. D. These remarks may suffice for the present; but on a future occasion, I shall treat more fully of this question.

Although Justi's Bundehesh contains some valuable information, a new edition in the Pahlavî character, with a more correct transliteration and glossary is wanted, to prevent the spread of so many groundless readings and meanings of Pahlavî words; and it gives me pleasure to state that my friend E. West will shortly undertake it, with my assistance, as I cannot as yet find the necessary leisure for carrying it out.

Among the Pahlavî texts published, besides the Bundehesh and the translations of the Vendidâd, Yasna and Visparad, I have to mention the old Zand-Pahlavî Glossary, published by Destur Hoshengji, at my recommendation and with my assistance, in 1867 [1]). I added two minor

1) An old Zand-Pahlavî Glossary. Edited in the original characters, with a transliteration in Roman letters, a translation and an alphabetical index by Destur Hoshengji Jamaspji. Revised, with notes and introduction, by M. Haug. Bombay and London, 1867.

Pahlavî texts, both bearing on the fate of the Zoroastrian writings in ancient times, viz. an extract from the Dîn-kart, and the beginning of the Ardâi-Virâf-nâmeh, with transliteration and translation. In the introduction, I made some remarks on the age, origin and character of the Pahlavi language, which I shall develop more fully and set in a clearer light in the present essay. I expressed my doubts as to the correctness of the current opinion, that it originated in the period immediately preceding the Sasanian kings, and showed the probability of its origin having to be sought in a much earlier portion of Iranian history. I likewise endeavoured to make some progress in the decipherment of the Hâjîâbâd inscriptions, and to show a probable connection between the Pahlavî and the Assyrian.

Let us now return to the inscriptional Pahlavî before concluding this historical sketch. In 1865, François Lenormant published, in the Journal asiatique (sixième série, tome VI. pag. 180—226), his Palæographic studies on the Pahlavî alphabet, its different varieties and its origin [1]). Referring to the researches of De Sacy, Olshausen, etc., into the Sasanian Pahlavî on coins and in inscriptions, and to the numismatic studies of the Duc de Luynes [2]) on the coins of the Satraps during the Achæmenian rule, and of E. Thomas on a certain class of Arsacid coins with Pahlavî legends [3]), he draws a very lucid and instructive sketch of the development of the Pahlavî alphabets from the Aramæan of the third period (B. C. 300—100). He distinguishes four varieties of the Pahlavî alphabet, discoverable on coins and monuments, viz. *a*) Proto-Pahlavî, on a certain class of Arsacid coins; *b*) Persepolitan Pahlavî, that used in the Hâjîâbâd inscription B, and similar versions of other bi-lingual inscriptions; *c*) Sasanian Pahlavî; and *d*) the Pahlavî of the MSS. The Proto-Pahlavî is

---

1) Études paléographiques sur l'alphabet Pehlevi, ses diverses variétés et son origine.

2) Essai sur la numismatique des Satrapies sous les rois Achæménides. 2 vols, Paris, 1846.

3) Numismatic Chronicle, vol. XII, pag. 68—77 and 91—114.

regarded by him as being nearest to the Palmyrenian branch of the Aramæan alphabet of the third period; but this intermediate step is not required, as the several characters can be derived, without difficulty, direct from the Aramæan of the later period, as can be readily seen on glancing at Lenormant's fourth table, 'origine de l'écriture Pehlevie'. He also gives some valuable notices, from the Paris MS. of the Kitâbu-l-fihrist, regarding the different kinds of writing used during the reign of the Sasanian dynasty.

Also bearing on the subject of the early use of Pahlavî writing in Persia, is a very interesting article by M. A. Levy, Professor at Breslau, published in 1867, in the Journal of the German Oriental Society (vol. XXI, pag. 421—465) under the title [1]: 'contributions to the Aramæan numismatics of Iran, and to a knowledge of the earlier Pahlavî writing'. He discusses the so-called sub-Parthian coins, meaning thereby the coins of local dynasties which existed and ruled in the East, under the shadow of the Arsacidan empire. He had a more extensive material to work upon than E. Thomas, his predecessor in these investigations, as the Duc de Luynes had placed at his disposal, impressions of all the coins of this class which are in his collection; he was, therefore, able to arrive at more satisfactory results. He has shown, and I believe on sufficient grounds, that these coins may be traced to the end of the fourth and beginning of the third century B. C.; that they were struck by Persian vassal kings, in the south, who were subject to Alexander and the Seleucidæ; that the characters found upon them closely resemble the Aramæan character of the third period; and that the kings who coined them were Ormazd-worshippers. The explanations he proposes, of the legends, must be taken as tentative; the principal legend on most of them, he reads פרתכרא זי אלה and translates by 'the image of the divine' (viz. of the king who is depicted on them). With the reading I quite agree, so far

1) Beiträge zur aramäischen Münzkunde Eran's und zur Kunde der ältern Pehlewi Schrift.

as I can judge from the figures given by him in a lithographed table; but I object to the translation of פרתכרא by 'image', which is *patikara* in old Persian, and not *prati-kara*, as the form פרתכרא would require; the *r* of the Sans. *prati*, being always wanting in Zand (*paiti*) and old Persian; besides, the term 'image' would be rather strange on a coin. It is, no doubt, an Iranian word, but means, very likely, 'worshipper' [1]), and with זי אלה, 'worshipper of God'; the king being actually represented on these coins, as praying to Ahura-mazda. The legend would thus be equivalent to the title *mazdayasn* on the Sasanian coins; and this is the more likely, as a royal name is often associated with it.

After discussing this very interesting and important class of coins, he treats of those Arsacidan coins which bear legends in Pahlavî characters, and finally makes some remarks on the Sasanian rock-inscriptions, but without advancing our knowledge of them to any considerable extent. Like Lenormant, he gives an instructive comparative table of the Pahlavî alphabets, the earliest of which he traces as far back as the fourth century B. C.

A most important service to the study of the Sasanian inscriptions, was rendered by E. Thomas, through the publication of his memoir on the 'Early Sasanian inscriptions, seals and coins (London, 1868)'. [2]) It contains the texts of all the Sasanian rock-inscriptions, in both kinds of Pahlavi characters, which are as yet known to exist in Persia, with partial attempts at translating and explaining them. The so-called **Pâî-Kûlî** inscriptions, of which Sir H. Rawlinson alone possessed copies, have been here published for the first time. The information he gives, regarding the Semitic alphabets, Phœnico-Babylonian and Ethiopian, of the time of Sargon (B. C. 721), the Aramæan and finally the Chaldæo-Pahlavî and

---

1) It may be traced to a supposed old Persian word *frathangra* (the *n* is not expressed before gutturals, in the cuneiform writing of ancient Persian documents), and this would have to be traced to *thah* = Z. *sah*, *saṅh* = Sans. *s'aṁs* 'to praise', and would mean 'praiser, worshipper'.

2) It first appeared in the Journal of the Royal Asiatic Society of Great Britain, New Series, vol. III. pag. 241—358.

Sasanian-Pahlavî alphabets, is very interesting. Regarding his readings, and still more his translations, considerable doubts may be raised, and in many cases they can be shown, on good grounds, to be erroneous. The author has too much neglected the Pahlavî of the books, which must be of the greatest service to the decipherer of the inscriptions, if its identity with the language of the latter can be proved, as appears to be the case. I need not enlarge here on this subject, as E. W. West has ably carried out my views regarding it, in an article of the latest number of the Journal of the R. A. S. (1869), headed 'Sasanian inscriptions explained by the Pahlavî of the Pârsîs'. Since Thomas does not lay claim to profound Pahlavî scholarship, but calls himself (pag. 72 of his memoir) only an 'amateur learner' who makes 'an independent search after knowledge', we cannot judge harshly of his shortcomings in so difficult a subject, and can only feel indignant at the vicious attack made upon him by one who, although laying claim to profound Zand and Pahlavî scholarship, has (as I have repeatedly shown) published grave errors, and proved himself in many respects, not as an independent scholar, but as a mere follower of Spiegel. Thomas has, on the whole, rendered more real service to the advance of our knowledge of Pahlavî, than his assailant, who has mainly propagated the views of others.

It was chiefly owing to the publication of Thomas's memoir, that I resumed my investigation of the Pahlavî inscriptions, especially those found at Hâjîâbâd, and of the character and nature of the Pahlavî language itself. A short abstract of the results I had arrived at (on the character of the Pahlavî language, with especial reference to the Sasanian inscriptions) was read by me, on the 6th February 1869, before the Royal Bavarian Academy of sciences, and published in the 'Sitzungsberichte' of that learned institution (1869 vol. I, pag. 86—118). [1]) The object of the present essay is to develop, more fully, the views I published in that article.

---

1) A short notice of the article appeared in Trübner's American and Oriental Record (February, 1869).

2. On the appellations 'Pahlavî' and 'Huzvâresh'.

The official language of the Sasanian dynasty is generally called Pahlavî [1]), and various interpretations of this word have been proposed. Anquetil derives it from the Persian *pahlû* پَهلو 'side'; and Pahlavî would accordingly mean 'the language of the frontier'. But although this opinion has been held by many scholars, it is certainly not correct, as it is difficult to imagine that a frontier language would have spread over a vast empire. As no suitable meaning can be obtained from *pahlû*, it has been traced to *pahlav*, which is also written پَهلو, but has very different meanings. According to the native Persian dictionary Farhang-i Jehângîrî (See Vullers, Lexicon Persico-Latinum vol. I. pag. 386), *pahlav* has the following meanings: *a*) a town; *b*) the environs of Ispahan; *c*) a courageous man; *d*) a man of rank; *e*) a province which has given its name to the Pahlavî language. To this the following remarks are added: 'Some say, it is that language which was spoken at the capital of the Kayanians; according to others, Pahlav was the name of a son of Shem, the son of Noah'. In the Farhang shu'ûri (see Vullers, l. c.), it is further explained, that the province, called Pahlav, comprised five towns, viz. Isfahân, Reî, Hamadân, Nehâvand and Adarbeijân [2]). No doubt, the five meanings assigned to *pahlav*, afford ample material for etymologists, and they have readily availed themselves of it. Native lexicographers have traced Pahlavî to *pahlav* 'town', according to which it would mean 'the language of towns'; but this is inadmissable, as it was just the

---

1) This subject has been discussed by Anquetil Duperron, in the 'Mémoires de l'Académie des inscriptions et belles-lettres', pag. 407—408; by Quatremère, in the 'Journal des Savants' for 1840, pag. 343—347; by Marc Jos. Müller, in an article 'Ueber den Namen Pehlvi', published in the 'Bulletin der K. bayerischen Akademie der Wissenschaften' for 1842, pag. 98—111; and by Spiegel, in his Huzvâresh grammar, pag. 16—20.

2) These notices have been taken from the writings of Hamza Isfahânî and Ibn Muqaffa; see Marc. Jos. Müller's article in the Bulletin der K. bayer. Akad. der Wissensch. for Sept. 1842, pag. 106.

village squire, the دِهقان 1), or دِهگان, who preserved the Pahlavî traditions in Persia, as we learn from Firdûsî's Shâhnâmeh. It has also been connected with *pahlavân* 'a hero', in which case it would be 'the language of heroes', which meaning is also open to objection.

The derivation of the word from Pahlav, as the name of a large district, is certainly preferable to any of the etymologies above mentioned. As that district comprised the ancient Media, Pahlavî would thus be the language of Media; but this country is never called Pahlav by Persian, or Arab, historians. Quatremère is of opinion that Pahlav was identical with the province Parthia, mentioned by the Greeks; he shows, by reference to Armenian authors, that *pahlav* was a royal title of the Arsacidæ, or the descendants of Arŝak the Great, the founder of the dynasty. As the Parthians regarded themselves as the most warlike people of the orient, it is not surprising that *pahlav* and *pahlavân* in Persian, and *palhav*, or *pahlav*, and *pahlavig*, or *palhavig* 2), in Armenian, became appellations for a warrior; the name thus lost its national meaning altogether, and became only a honorary title for bold champions of old. The name spread beyond the frontiers of Iran, eastwards to the Indians; for we find the Pahlavâs, as a mighty foreign nation, mentioned in the

---

1) This is the Arabic orthography, as the word is also used in Arabic, though borrowed from the Persian; with regard to its meaning, see Vullers Lexicon Pers.-Lat. vol. I. pag. 942; and Jawâlîqî's Almuarrab, ed. Sachau (1867) pag. 65 of the Arabic text.

2) The Armenian writers derive this word from the town of Bahl, Bahgh, i. e. Balkh which is stated, by Moses of Chorene, to have been the residence of Arshak the Great (Arsaces, the founder of the Arsacidan dynasty); see his 'Armenian History' Venice edition of 1843, pag. 148, and Quatremère in the Journal des Savants of 1840, pag. 345. This is apparently only owing to the similarity of sound in *pahlav*, and *bahl*; but there is still a distinction marked by the initial letter; when *bahl* means the town of Balkh it is not written with an initial *p*, and in like manner, *pahlavig* 'a royal prince, a hero', is not written with *b*. The words, *pahlava* and *balhika* (*bâlhika, bâlhîka*) are also distinguished in Sanscrit. The name of *balhika* occurs already in the Atharveda-Samhitâ (5, 22, 7. 9.) where it signifies the Bactrians, as well as in later times. I make these remarks only to caution against a derivation of Pahlavî from Balkh, as has been ventured upon by Dr. Mordtmann in the Zeitschrift der D. Morg. Ges. vol. XIX, pag. 413.

Râmâyana, Mahâbhârata and the Laws of Manu, and we can only understand them to be the Persians. Regarding the origin of the word, we may connect it with [illegible] *pahalûm* 'excellent', but cannot derive it therefrom.

As the name of a nation, we can discover it only in the Parthva of the cuneiform inscriptions, which is the Parthia of the Greeks and Romans. The change of *parthva* to *pahlav* is not surprising, as *l* is not discoverable in the ancient Iranian tongues and *r* is always found in its stead; *th* in the middle of a word generally becomes *h*, comp. Z. *mithra*, Pers. مهر. It may be objected that the Parthians were not Persians, but probably a Scythic race, and that Pahlavî could not have been the language of the Parthians. This objection, however, will not hold good, when we consider that the Parthians were, for nearly five hundred years, the actual rulers of Persia, and made themselves respected and famous everywhere, by their fierce and successful contests with the mightiest nation of the ancient world, the Romans. It is, therefore, not surprising that the name, which once struck such terror into the hearts of Roman generals and emperors, was retained in Persia, and that everything connected with antiquity, such as history, religion, letters, writing and language, was called پهلوی *pahlavî*, i. e. ancient, belonging to the ancient rulers of the country, the Parthians. Pahlavî thus means, in fact, nothing but 'ancient Persian' in general, without restriction to any particular dialect. This we may see from the use made of the word by the later Mohamedan writers; thus, Ibn Hauqal, an Arab geographer of the tenth century, states, when describing the province of Fârs, the ancient Persis, that three languages were used there, viz. *a*) the Fârsî (Persian) spoken by the natives when conversing with one another, which was spread all over Persia, and understood everywhere; *b*) the Pahlavî, which was the language of the ancient Persians, in which the Magi wrote their historical records, but which in the writer's time could not be understood by the inhabitants of the province, without a translation; *c*) the Arabic, which was used for all official documents. Of other languages spoken in Persia, he notices the Khûzî, the language of Khûzistân, which he states to be quite different from Hebrew, Syriac, or Fârsî [1]). In the **Mujmilu-t-tewârikh** (Journ. Asiat. April 1841, pag. 346), there is an interesting statement regarding the inscriptions at Persepolis, which must be those in cuneiform characters, although they are called 'Pahlavî' [2]).

From all this, we may clearly see that the name Pahlavî was not limited to any particular period, or district. In the time of Firdûsî (A. D. 1000), the cuneiform writing, as well as the Sasanian and Chaldæo-Pahlavî, passed for Pahlavî character; and the ancient Persian and the Zand were regarded as Pahlavî, equally with the official language of the Sasanian period, to which the term has been now restricted, since the others have become better known. The term Pahlavî was thus, in fact, never used by

---

1) See **Quatremère**, Journal des Savants for 1840, pag. 411—412. The Khûzî is in all probability the language of the second class of the Achæmenian inscriptions, as has been already pointed out by Dr. Mordtmann, in his very able article on this class of cuneiform writing, in the Zeitschrift der D. M. G. vol. XVI.

2) I give here a translation of the passage (the original Persian will be found in the Journal Asiatique quoted above): 'And at this place (هزار ستون = Persepolis) there are writings in Pahlavî. They say, that once upon a time, they called a Mobed to read them; *in summa* the contents were these: 'Jam has made this at this time, in such a month and such a day'; and the Pahlavî writing contains these words and many others; I did not copy them because I did not understand the character, which does not represent any other shape but that of plaitings (كه از صورت غرضى بر نخيزد); they call the place *hazâr setûn*, i. e. a thousand pillars'. This description of the writing clearly shows that the author was referring to the cuneiform writings, and not to the few Pahlavî inscriptions which are found there. That the cuneiform inscriptions of Persepolis excited the interest of some Arab rulers of Persia, and that they were anxious to know their meaning, we learn from the Arabic and Persian inscriptions to be found there, and which have been read and explained by De Sacy, in his 'Mémoires sur des diverses antiquités de la Perse' (pag. 125—165). One of the Arabic inscriptions, in the Kufic character, runs as follows (Mem. pag. 137): 'The Emir **Abu-Shoja Adhad-ed-daula** has seen this, in the month of Safar of the three hundred and forty-fourth year (A. D. 955), and the writing which is on these ruins has been read to him. Ali, the son of Alserri, the Kurdish writer, and Mar Said, the Mobed of Kazerun, read it'. Perhaps the statement of the **Mujmil** refers to the same circumstance; but the Emir was no doubt deceived by the writer and mobed, when they professed to read the characters which they cannot be supposed to have understood.

the Persians themselves, in any other sense than that of 'ancient Persian', whether they referred to the Sasanian, or Arsacidan, or Achæmenian, or Kayanian, or Peshdadian times. Any reader of the Shâhnâmeh will arrive at this conclusion.

The meaning of the term Huzvâresh, which is frequently applied to Pahlavî, is more difficult to settle. The earliest passage in which the word occurs (but in the form زوارش *zevâresh*) is to be found in the Kitâbu-l-fihrist of Mohamed ben Isḥaq, who has taken this, as well as his other statements regarding the seven kinds of writing used by the Persians of the Sasanian and ante-Sasanian times [1]), from Ibn Muqaffa, a Mohamedan writer of the latter half of the eighth century, who was of a very inquisitive mind (like Mas'ûdî who lived two centuries after him), and asked for information from the most learned priests, as appears from the notices which have been published regarding him [2]). His statements seem, therefore, to be well-authenticated and deserving of full credit. It is, on this account, much to be regretted that all the passages from his work, relating to the languages and alphabets of Iran, have not yet been published in full, in their original language.

The important passage relating to Huzvâresh, was first given to the world by Quatremère, in his excellent essay on the Nabathæans (Journal asiatique for 1835, vol. 15, pag. 256), but only in a French translation, without the original Arabic text. The honor of having published the latter for the first time, belongs to Charles Ganneau (Journal asiatique for 1866, vol. 7, pag. 430), and he has also made some critical remarks on Quatremère's translation, showing that it was not sufficiently accurate to prevent wrong inferences from being drawn. As the passage is of paramount importance for judging of the true character of the so-called Huzvâresh language, I give it here in full, with a translation of my own.

---

1) Quatremère, Journal des savants for 1840, pag. 415—416. The passage has also been quoted (from Quatremère) by Spiegel, in the introduction to his Huzvâresh grammar.

2) See, besides the articles of Quatrèmere, Lenormant, Journal asiatique for 1865 (Sixième série, tome VI. pag. 197—199).

ولهم هجاء يقال له زوارش يكتبون بها الحروف موصول
ومفصول وهو نحو الف كلمة ليفصلوا بها بين المتشابهات
مثال ذلك انّه من اراد ان يكتب كوشت وهو اللحم بالعربية
كتب بِسْرًا وتقراه كوشت على هذا المثال واذا اراد ان
يكتب نان وهو الخبز بالعربية كتب لَهْمًا وتقراه نان على
هذا المثال وعلى هذا كل شى ارادوا ان يكتبوه الا
اشيا لا يحتاج الى قلبها تكتب على اللفظ

Translation. 'They (the Persians) possess also a kind of spelling which they call *zevâresh;* they write by it the characters connected as well as separated (i. e. the characters appear sometimes joined, sometimes separated). It consists of about a thousand words (which are put together) in order to distinguish those which have the same meaning [1]). For instance, if somebody intends to write *gosht*, that is meat (*lakhm*) in Arabic, he writes *bisrâ*, but reads *gosht*, according to this example ; and if somebody intends to write *nân*, that is bread (*khubz*) in Arabic, he writes *lahmâ*, but reads *nân*, according to this example . And in this manner they treat all words that they intend to write. Only things which do not require such a change, are written just as they are pronounced'.

This passage, although it appears simple enough at first sight, requires some explanation. Quatremère translates هِجَاء by 'alphabet'; but Ganneau objects to this, and I think on good grounds. The author of the Kitâbu-l-fihrist introduces his information, on the different alphabets existing in Persia, by noticing that 'there are seven kinds of writing (خطّ) in Persia'; and after decribing seven kinds of alphabets, he then adds this notice on Huzvâresh. Had he considered it as an alphabet, he would have stated at first that there were 'eight', and not 'seven', alphabets in Persia.

---

1) Thus I translate متشابهات, as the meaning can hardly be otherwise than indicating that in the Pahlavî-Pâzand Glossary, which is evidently here alluded to (see pag. 39—40), each Semitic word has its Persian equivalent attached, by which it is read. It cannot refer to words which are written alike, or in a similar way.

Besides, the Arabic word هِجَاء does not mean 'alphabet', which is expressed by حُرُوفُ آلْهِجَاء, but هِجَاء is explained by the Turkish Qâmûs as follows: الهجاء كساء وزننده بر لفظی حروفيله تقطيع ايلمك معناسنه در 'the meaning of *hijâ*, which is formed and declined like *kisâ*, is this: to break up a word into its (several) letters'. As the Arabic alphabet omits the short vowels in writing, and each حرف, or letter, therefore represents a syllable, we can only define *hijâ* as 'spelling'. Ibn Muqaffa certainly did not understand any alphabet by it, as is clearly shown by his detailed description of the practical application of this *zevâresh*, which is of the highest interest, and from which we must infer that he meant the substitution of Persian words in reading, for the foreign and strange-sounding ones that appeared in writing. The correctness of this statement can be ascertained from the fact (to which I have, on several occasions, directed the attention of European scholars) that the Parsi priests of the present day, read the Semitic portion of the Pahlavî exactly in the manner indicated. For instance, they never read [illegible] *yetîbûntan* (to sit) as the letters actually sound, but always pronounce it *nishastan*, which is its Persian equivalent; but the Persian words in the Pahlavî, they read just as they are written, and this is also indicated in Ibn Muqaffa's statement, by the words: 'only things which do not require such a change, are written just as they are pronounced'.

This *zevâresh* is further stated, by Ibn Muqaffa, to consist of 'about a thousand words', which is also contrary to the definition of *hijâ* as 'alphabet'; for all the Pahlavî alphabets, according to his own showing, consist of a much smaller number of letters, even if all the compound characters were counted; the highest number of letters, according to him, is only 40; but in a Rivâyat at my disposal, there are 41. So large a number as 'a thousand words' would induce the student to understand by *zevâresh* a kind of vocabulary; and in fact, such a vocabulary is still extant and called the Sasanian Farhang, which is the same as is published in this volume, for the first time in its primitive order, by Destur Hoshengji, and which actually consists of about a thousand words, if the appendices are deducted [1]). It is arranged exactly as one might expect from Ibn Muqaffa's statement; first comes a foreign word which is generally Semitic, though sometimes modified Persian, and this is always followed by its ordinary Persian equivalent; it also contains the very words which are quoted, as examples, by Ibn Muqaffa, thus *lahmâ* = *nân* [Pahlavi] . [Pahlavi] occurs in 3, 6. and *bisrâ* = *gosht* [Pahlavi] . [Pahlavi] occurs in 6, 9. We can hardly therefore be wrong in assuming that the Farhang here published, was that one known to Ibn Muqaffa, and must therefore have existed, as an old work, in the eighth century.

Let us sum up what Ibn Muqaffa meant by *zevâresh.* It is according to him a peculiar way of writing and pronouncing; that is, a foreign word was really written, but its Persian equivalent was always pronounced in its stead; but this strange proceeding was confined to a certain number of words, contained in a list or vocabulary, in which words having the same meaning were put together, the foreign word (generally Semitic) being written alongside its Persian equivalent. This peculiar way of writing and pronouncing a limited number of words, can by no means be called a language; so that a Huzvâresh language does not exist, according to Ibn Muqaffa.

The question now arises, whence is this word *zevâresh* to be derived. Its identity with *czvârsh* in Pâzand, and *huzvârashna* [Pahlavi] or [Pahlavi] in Pahlavî, can hardly be denied. We may take [Pahlavi] as the more primitive form. It occurs in a gloss of the Sasanian Farhang (pag. 17) which runs thus: [Pahlavi] [Pahlavi] [Pahlavi] [Pahlavi] [Pahlavi] [Pahlavi]; this is the amended reading of Destur Hoshengjî, but the MSS. read [Pahlavi] instead of [Pahlavi] [Pahlavi]. If we adhere to the reading of the MSS., it must be translated thus: 'as regards writing, in

1) The older part of the glossary, as it now stands (pag. 1—19 of the Pahlavî text), contains 1023 words, including the Pâzand; 27 of these are repetitions, but many of them unavoidable; so that the original glossary must have contained, as nearly as possible, 1000 words. The appendices (pag. 19—24) are evidently later additions.

Huzvâresh *yektîbûntan* is to write': but although this remark is quite correct, it is very strange to find it in a list of verbs, in which the Huzvâresh verb is, in all other instances, explained merely by a Persian verb being placed in juxta-position, and without a single additional explanatory word; the clause [Pahlavi] would have been quite sufficient, and in conformity with all the rest. The passage in the MSS. is no doubt corrupt, and the Destur's emendation is preferable; so that the meaning is: 'as regards writing, *yektîbûntan* (to write) is not used in Huzvâresh for *napeshtan*'; that is to say, in writing Huzvâresh, the word *yektîbûntan*, which is the proper term for 'writing', is not employed, but the Persian *napeshtan* is retained. And, indeed, [Pahlavi] *nipishtî*, 'written', is more frequently found in the inscriptions than [Pahlavi] *yektîbûn*; the former occurs at Naksh-i Rajab, lin. 22. 31. and at Naksh-i Rustam, lin. 8., while I have found the latter only once, at Naksh-i Rajab, lin. 25; the same may be observed to be the case in the Dîn-kart.

With regard to the form of the word [Pahlavi] *huzvârashn*, or [Pahlavi] *huzvânashn* as Destur Hoshengji says it is sometimes written, it is clearly an abstract noun formed with the suffix *eshn*, like *bundeheshn* 'beginning'. Now such a noun can scarcely be the name of a particular language, as that would be expressed by some adjective, but it means a 'method of writing', as we have also seen is the case with the word *zevâresh*. But we have other proofs that it does not mean a language. In Pahlavî books we find frequently the notice: [Pahlavi] 'I write (this) in Huzvârashn', that is, in the peculiar method according to which a Persian word is read for each foreign one. In one of Anquetil's MSS. (VII, fonds, pag. 106) there is the remark: نه در کلام مانثر و نه در ازوارش و نه در کلام بزرگان دین و نه در کتابهای اهل فرس 'neither in the language of the Mânthra (Avesta = Zand), nor in Ezvâresh, nor in the language of the chiefs of the religion (Pârsî), nor in the books of the Persian people'; here Zand and Pârsî are called languages, and Persian books are spoken of, but Ezvâresh has no such denomination; if the author had considered it as a language, he would have added the word كلام, but it was to him a kind of orthography, or writing. Another Pâzand passage, which proves the same, is also found in another of Anquetil's MSS. (VI, fonds, pag. 94): [1]) *ba khata awstâ, yâ khata sevât avâit navēsht kē uzvârsh*, 'it is to be written in the writing of the Avesta, or in that of Sevât which is *uzvârsh*'; here *uzvârsh* is taken as the writing of Sevât (Sevad), i. e. Chaldæa, but by no means as a language. The only passage, known to me, which might be quoted to show that Huzvâresh was the name of a language, occurs in Anquetil's modified copy of the Pahlavî-Pâzand glossary (see Zend-Avesta, tome II, pag. 523), where we find the phrase: *yektîbûnam benâ lîsân huzvâreshn*, 'I write in the Huzvâresh language'; but this is, no doubt, merely a gloss written by Destur Dârâb, who re-arranged the glossary, in an alphabetical form, for Anquetil (as appears from the colophon, pag. 525—526), and therefore only represents the opinion of some Pârsî priests about a century ago.

Though there can now be little doubt as to the meaning of **Huzvâresh**, its etymology is by no means easily discovered. Destur Hoshengji explains it as *huzvân-asôr*, 'the language of Assyria', an interpretation which I had also adopted before examining the actual use of the word [2]); but this can no longer be entertained. Some scholars trace it to the Zand *huzvârena* (Yasht 5, 6. ed. Westergaard), but that reading is very doubtful, as almost all the MSS. differ, and its meaning is also quite uncertain; it would therefore be unsafe to base any etymology upon it. But even supposing the meaning 'good power, strength' (which has been attached to it, by a mere etymological guess) were correct, what

---

1) These passages are taken from Marc Jos. Müller's paper, on the name of Pahlavî, in the Bulletin der K. bayer. Akademie der Wissenschaften for Sept. 1842, pag. 102.

2) I had followed the current opinion that *huzvâresh* is a language, and taking it as such, I sought for a reasonable explanation. The simplest etymology which presented itself to the Destur and myself, was to take the word as a corruption of  *huzvân asôr*; but I was fully aware that an original *n* is never changed to *r*.

possible connection could it have with *huzvâresh*, whose proper meaning is, as we have seen, a peculiar mode of writing and pronouncing? That *huzvâresh* is to be traced to an Aryan root, there can be little doubt. The first syllable هوز is very likely only the preposition *uz* = Sans. *ut* (ه being only a so-called *mater lectionis* and not to be pronounced, or it may be a later addition, comp. Pers. هیزم 'wood', Z. *aêsma*); the second syllable *var* must then be the root, and *esh*, or *eshn*, the abstract suffix. If we trace it to *var* 'to choose, select', the word would mean 'selection, choice', but this would be no appropriate meaning for *huzvâresh;* if we take *var* 'to cover', as the root, *uz* + *varesh* would mean 'uncovering, revelation', which is also unsuitable. More probably it has some connection with the Sanskrit *varṇa* 'a letter', which has that meaning in such early works as the Prâtis'âkhyas (see the Prâtis'âkhya of the Rigveda I. 9. 10.); in that case, the word might mean 'spelling, pronouncing', which would agree very well with the meaning of *huzvâresh*. With this I rest satisfied, till a better etymology is found.

3. The Sasanian inscriptions deciphered.

Since the languages found in the inscriptions which the kings of the Sasanian dynasty have left in Persia, must form the basis on which any sound opinion, regarding the character and nature of the Pahlavî language, can alone be founded, it will be necessary to attempt deciphering at least one of the longer inscriptions as completely as possible. I am fully aware that it is an arduous task to decipher, for the first time, an inscription which has as yet baffled all attempts, and has been unintelligible for centuries; but I have never shrunk from difficulties, if I could render any real service to the advance of knowledge [1]), though it is an ungrateful

1) I may be permitted here to instance my work on the Gâthas, and my edition and translation of the Aitareya Brâhmana. The former was the *first* attempt to give a full explanation of the most difficult and (as regards the origin of the Zoroastrian religion) the most important portion of the Zand-avesta; although it is

undertaking to pave the way for others. Fifteen years ago I made the first attempt to go a little beyond De Sacy, by deciphering some words of the Hâjîâbâd inscriptions; two years ago I made another advance, but it was only this year, that I was able to venture upon a tentative translation of a whole text, after having settled, to my own satisfaction, the meanings of most of the words, so that no doubt could be entertained as to the general tenor of the inscription. In my attempt I was greatly assisted by Thomas's Essay on early Sasanian inscriptions, and by my friend E. W. West who is a skilful palæographer. He prepared for me a transcript of the Hâjîâbâd inscriptions according to Westergaard's copy and the photograph given by Thomas, and placed at my disposal, an alphabetical index of all the words which can be read with any degree of certainty in all the known Sasanian inscriptions.

The Sasanian alphabet, with which the greater number of the inscriptions are inscribed, is as follows: *â*, *b*, *g*, *d*, *h*, *kh*, *v*, *û*, *r*, *z*, *y*, *î*, *k*, *l*, *r*, *m*, *n*, *s*, *p*, *f*, *ch*, *sh*, *t*; and besides these seventeen letters, there are two compound characters *man* and *kat*. In transliterating the Sasanian words, I shall use the letters attached to each of these characters, and where they have more than one phonetic value, that one will be used which best accords with the orthography of the word in the cognate languages. The vowels *A*, *â*, *î* and *û* are expressed by the Sasanian characters , and ; but the vowels *a*, *i* and *u*, without a circumflex, are not expressed in the original character, but are added to facilitate pronunciation, and in accordance with the etymology of the word. The phonetic value of the character has been thought to be *î*, chiefly on

nothing final, but would admit of great improvement, our knowledge of the Gâthas has not advanced, in the slightest degree, since its publication, but has been brought into a complete state of confusion by Spiegel, his transcriber Justi, and their common follower Kossowitsch. The question whether the Gâthas contain sense, or not, seems to be now considered of little importance, so long as due attention is paid to the etymologies of old Desturs, however absurd they may be.

account of its resemblance, in form, to the Zand letter ; but its identity with the Pahlavî is sufficiently proved by its occurrence as the final character in the words *barman* = , *hûman* = , *zanman* = , *ûlman* = and eight others that are readily identified [1]). The phonetic value of the compound character is known only from its occurring twice, as the initial character in the word *katab*. — Of the Chaldæo-Pahlavî inscriptions, I cannot give the alphabet, which contains 19 characters, for want of the necessary type.

a) The Hâjîâbâd inscriptions [2]).

I commence with the Hâjîâbâd inscriptions of Sapor I. (238—269 A. D.), as we possess better copies of them than of any of the other inscriptions of any length. They are two in number, one in the so-called Sasanian and the other in the Chaldæo-Pahlavî [3]) character; the former is marked A, the latter B, by Westergaard. They are found engraved on the rock-wall at the entrance of a cave near Hâjîâbâd, a village which is at no great distance from Persepolis; no sculptures have been discovered at the same place, but if there were any, they might be of great assistance to the decipherer.

1) For a fuller discussion of this subject, see the Zand-Pahlavî Glossary, pag. XXI, and E. W. West's 'Sassanian Inscriptions explained by the Pahlavî of the Parsis', in the Journal of the Roy. As. Soc.

2) Copies of these inscriptions will be found in Ker Porter's Travels, vol. I, pag. 513; in Westergaard's Bundehesh, pag. 83--84; in Flandin's Voyage en Perse, vol. IV, pl. 193; and in Thomas's 'Sasanian Inscriptions', Journal of the Roy. As. Soc. new series, vol. III, pag. 241. Of these, the first and third are of little use to the decipherer.

3) I adopt these terms, which have been used by Mr. Thomas, for the sake of convenience. Others propose for the Sasanian Pahlavî, the expression, east-Pahlavî, and for the Chaldæo-Pahlavî, that of west-Pahlavî.

8. The Sasanian text of A is as follows:

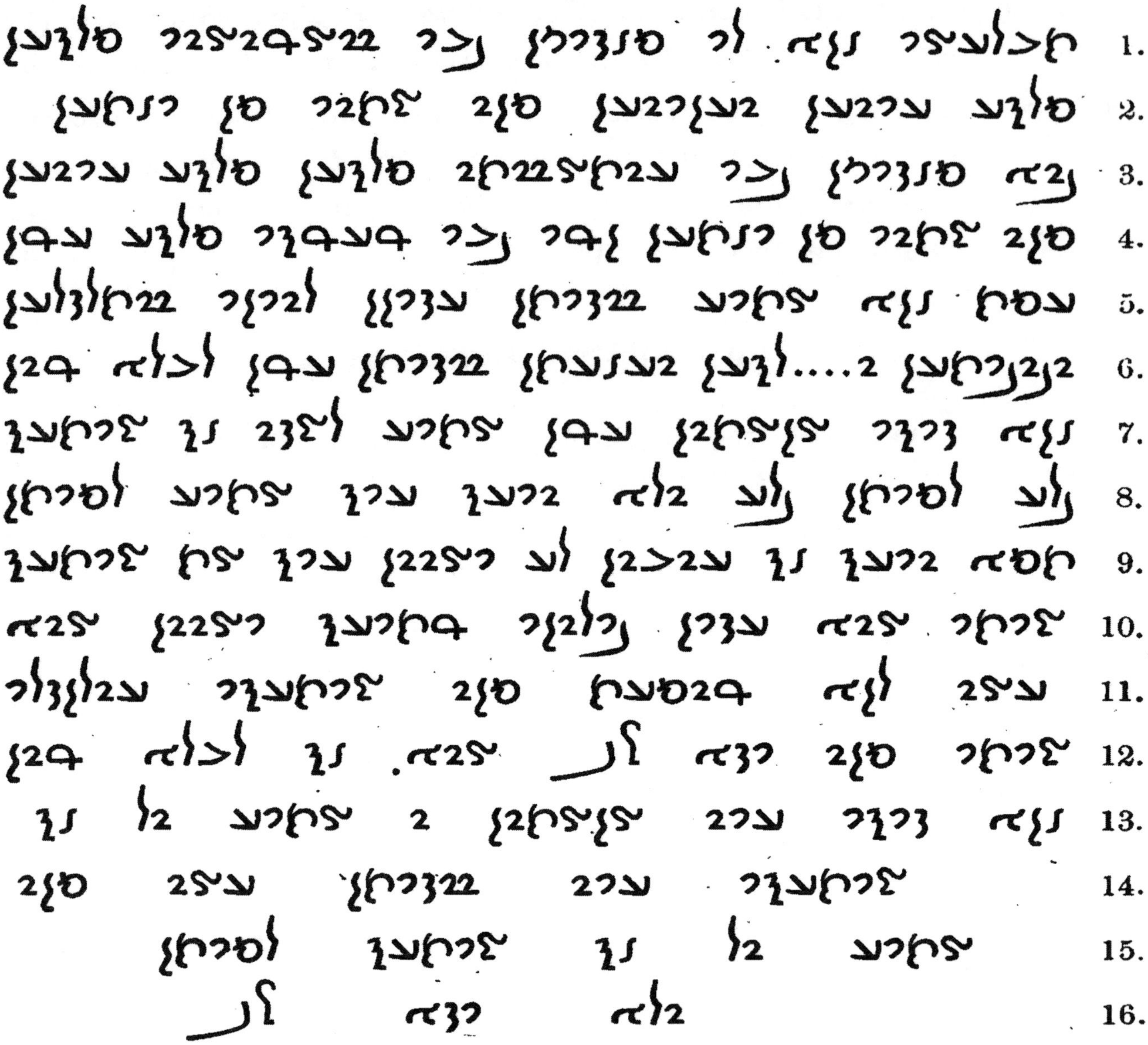

8. Transliteration of A.

1. *Tagalâhî zanman li mazdayasn bagî Shahpûhrî malkân*
2. *malkâ Aîrân û Anîrân minû chitrî min yaztân*
3. *barman mazdayasn bagî Artakhshatr malkân malkâ Aîrân*
4. *minû chitrî min yaztân napî bagî Pâpakî malkâ âpan*
5. *âmat zanman hatyâ shadîtun âdînan lûînî shatardarân*

6. *û barbîtân û . . lkân û âzâtan shadîtun âpan ragalman pavan*
7. *zanman dîkî hanakhtûn âpan hatyâ lachadû zak chîtâk*
8. *barâ ramîtun barâ ûlman vayâk âik hatyâ ramîtun*
9. *tamman vayâk zak ârgûn lâ yahvûn âik hat chîtâk*
10. *chîtî hûman âdîn bîrûnî patyâk yahvûn hûman*
11. *âkhar lanman*] *armât minû chîtâkî âûlandalî*
12. *chîtî minû yadman katab hûman zak ragalman pavan*
13. *zanman dıkî âyû hanakhtûn û hatyâ ûl zak*
14. *chîtâkî âyû shadîtun âkhar minû*
15. *hatyâ ûl zak chîtâk ramîtun*
16. *ûlman yadman katab*

Ch. Transliteration of B.

1. *karzâvanî zanman lî mazdayazn âlahâ Şhahîpûhar*
2. *malkîn malkâ Aryân û Anâryân minû shîhar min*
3. *yâztan barî mazdayazn âlahâ Artakhshatr malkîn malkâ*
4. *Aryân minû shîhar min yâztan pûhrî-pûhar bag Pâpak*
5. *malkâ û âmat lan zanman hararyâ shadît qadmatman khshatardarîn*
6. *barbîtân rabân û âzâtan shadît nagarîn pavîn (patan) zak vîm*
7. *haqâîmût û hararyâ lahad lehû shîtî lebarâ ramît bîsh*
8. *tamman ânû hararyâ napalt lehavînd âtarman lâ yehût âik*
9. *âk shîtî banît havîndî kal lebarâ shaddrâ ârqî yehût*
10. *havîndî âdîn lan âûpdasht minû shîtî panman qatar*
11. *banît âvat minû yadâ kadab havînt nagarîn pavîn (patan)*
12. *zanman vîm hîp haqâîmûd û hararyâ kal hû*
13. *shîtî hîp shadyû minû hararyâ kal hûp shîtî*
14. *yâmzûd lehûp yadâ kadab havîndî*

Commentary.

Lin. 1. S. [Pahlavi] *tagalâhî*, Ch. *karzâvanî*. As to the correctness of the reading of *tagalâhî*, there can hardly be any doubt, as the letters are quite clear and distinct in W.'s copy, and it is not contradicted by the photograph, in which only the two letters [Pahlavi] are somewhat indistinct. Instead of *karzâvanî*, E. West reads *karzâvâ;* but in W.'s copy the last *â* is dissolved into two letters which represent *nî;* in the photograph also there are traces of two letters visible after *karzâv*, which very probably represent *nî*. As both texts have the same meaning, *tagalâhî* and *karzâvanî* must be equivalent terms, and both have apparently to be traced to a Semitic source. *Karzâvanî* can only be derived from the Chaldee כְּרַז 'to proclaim'; *van* is a nominal suffix, probably identical with [Pahlavi] *man*, as *v* is not distinguished from *m* in Assyrian (see the index, pag. 194); *î* is the terminating vowel which so frequently occurs in the inscriptional Pahlavî (comp. *tagalâhî*, *bagî* in A., *shahîpûhar* in B.); the whole means evidently 'proclamation, edict'. As a root *tagar*, *tagal*, does not give any sense, *tagalâhî* must be traced to a root *nagal*, *nagar* (*r* and *l* being frequently interchanged in Pahlavî), which I identify with the Ethiopian *nagara* 'to speak, recite, relate', *nagar* 'a speech, an exposition', *tanâgârî* 'an orator'; the *t* prefixed to a verbal root, or to a modification of the root, denotes an abstract noun in the Semitic languages [1]), and verbs with *n* as the first radical (the so-called פ"נ) occasionally drop this letter, when ת is prefixed, as for instance in Hebrew, we have תְּקוּפָה 'circuit, revolution', from הִקִּיף 'to revolve' (Hifil of נקף) [2]). The original form of *tagalâhî* seems to have been *tagarâ*, instead of

1) Compare Chald. תּוֹכָחָא 'chastisement', from יְכַח 'to chastise'; Hebr. תְּשׁוּעַ 'help, salvation', from יָשַׁע 'to help'; Assyr. *taldit* 'birth', from *'alad* 'to generate'; etc.

2) This is certainly the correct derivation of the word, as given by Professor Ewald in his 'Ausführliche Lehrbuch der hebraischen Sprache' 6th edit. pag. 362. Gesenius derives it from a root קוף which, however, does not exist in the Semitic languages.

tangarâ; hî is no suffix, but *h* is only the guttural which follows final vowels in Pahlavi words, and in the books is generally represented by *k*, and *î* is similar to the *î* in *karzâvanî*.

S. *zanman*, Ch. id.; demonstrative pronoun, P. *denman* 'this', (see index, pag. 110.)

S. *lî*, Ch. id., P. ; 1st personal pronoun sing. 'I', Chald. לִי 'to me', (see index, pag. 189—190).

S. *mazdayasn*, Ch. *mazdayazn*, P. *mahêst* (see index, pag. 152), Z. *mazdayasna*, 'an Ormazd-worshipper, a Zoroastrian'.

S. *bagî*, Ch. *âlahâ*; 'god', *θεός*. This has been taken as an adjective, whenever it occurs among the titles of the Sasanian kings, in their inscriptions; but the equivalent *âlahâ*, in B., is against its being so understood; for this latter is clearly a substantive, meaning 'god', Chald. אֱלָהּ, אֱלָהָא, Hebr. אֱלוֹהַּ, אֱלֹהִים, Arab. إِلَاهٌ, إِلَهٌ, Syr. ܐܠܗܐ; if it were an adjective, we might expect *âlahî*, as אֱלָהִי in Chaldee really means 'divine'. In *bagî*, the *î* is no adjectival termination, but the vowel so frequently found at the end of Pahlavî words (see *karzâvanî*, pag. 48); on coins the *î* is frequently omitted, and also in Ch. lin. 4; *bag* itself is the *baga* of the Persian cuneiform inscriptions, Z. *baga*, meaning 'god'. If the Sasanian kings styled themselves *bag*, 'god', it is no more than the Seleucidæ did, when they assumed the title *θεός*.

S. *Shahpûhrî*, Ch. *Shahîpûhar;* the name of the king Shâpûr or Sapor. The form in Ch. differs from that in S., by placing the *î* after the first, instead of the second part of the word; the original form was, no doubt, *khshathra-puthra*, i. e. 'prince'. The king referred to, was Sapor I: who reigned A. D. 238—269.

S. *malkân* [lin. 2.] *malkâ*, Ch. *malkîn malkâ*, 'king of the kings', Pers. شاهنشاه, old Pers. *khshayathiya khshayathiyânâm.* This has been the title of the Persian kings from the most ancient times. That the words *malkân malkâ* admit of no other interpretation than 'king of kings', has been clearly proved by Mordtmann (Zeitschrift der D. M. G. vol. XIX, pag. 405—409). The word *malkâ* is Semitic, Chald. מַלְכָּא, and so also is the plural termination *în*; the Semitic character of the plural termination *ân* will be hereafter discussed.

S. *Aîrân û Anîrân*, Ch. *Aryân u Anâryân*, 'Iran and Aniran, i. e. Turân'. In Ch. the original forms are better preserved; they must have been *airyana* 'the country of the Airyas' (Aryans), and *anairyana* 'the country of the non-Airyas' (non-Aryans); *û* is the Semitic copulative particle, Hebr. וְ, Arab. وَ.

S. *minû-chitrî*, Ch. *minû-shîhar*, 'of spiritual origin'; in the Greek versions ἐκγενους (see pag. 4). *Minû*, Z. *mainyu*, Pers. مينو, is a peculiar Zoroastrian expression, with which we frequently meet in this inscription. The Parsi priests generally explain it by 'invisible'; and the term may be used of all things which exist, as it denotes the ideal, or celestial, existence of any thing whatever, as contrasted with its real existence, the visible object. Thus they speak of a *mînû zamîk*, 'an invisible earth', lit. 'a spirit-earth', of 'an invisible river', lit. 'a spirit-river', etc.; it does not mean the spirit of the thing, but only its spiritual, invisible existence, simultaneous with its material existence. *Chitrî*, Z. *chithra*, Pers. چهر, is 'seed'; and the whole compound means 'one whose seed (origin) is spiritual'.

S. *min yaztân*, Ch. *min yâztan*, 'from God'; for *yaztân* = *yazdân*, see index, pag. 235; *min* = מִן 'from'.

Lin. 3. S. *barman*, Ch. *barî*, 'son', Chald. בַּר, P. which must also be read *barman*.

S. *Artakhshatr*, Ch. id., 'Artaxerxes, Ardeshîr', the father of Shâpûr.

Lin. 4. S. *napî*, Ch. *pûhrîpûhar*, 'grandson'. Both terms are Aryan; *napî* is the old-Pers. *napâ*, Z. *napât*, nom. *napô*, *napâo*, Sans. *napât*, Lat. *nepos*; *pûhrîpûhar* is 'son of the son' (*pûhar* = old Pers. and Z. *puthra*, Sans. *putra*), *î* being a connecting vowel.

S. Pâpakî, Ch. *Pâpak*, the name of the father of Ardeshîr, from whom he is styled Bâbegân, 'the Pâpakan, or descendant of Pâpak'; P.

S. *âpan*, Ch. *û lan*, 'we, also we'. Here the difficulties commence; I had first identified *âpan* with ابر, but this is only the Persian او, or آن, which would not give any intelligible sense. The word occurs also in lin. 6 and 7, always at the beginning of a clause in the sentence, but in the two latter instances it is not fully rendered in the Chaldæo-Pahlavî version. In lin. 4—5, the sentence commences in S. with: *âpan âmat zanman hatyâ shadîtun*, which is rendered in Ch. as follows: *û âmat lan zanman hararyâ shadît*. Now *âpan* cannot correspond to *û* alone, the meaning of which is 'and', as may be seen from lin. 2 and 6; for if we made that assumption we should leave the Ch. *lan* without any equivalent in S.; *âmat* and *zanman* are alike in both versions, S. *hatyâ* is Ch. *hararyâ*, and S. *shadîtun* is Ch. *shadît*, consequently *âpan* must correspond to the remaining *û lan* in Ch.; *lan* occurs again in Ch. lin. 10, but as an equivalent of S. *lanman* = 'we'. The *âpan* in S. lin. 7, is in a similar position to *û* in Ch. lin. 7, but the *âpan* in S. lin. 6 has no corresponding word in Ch.; as the three clauses commencing with *âpan* in S., are closely connected and have the same subject, it is not surprising that the subject is expressed only once in Ch., by *lan* in the first clause. If we analyse *âpan*, the first syllable *âp* must correspond to *û*, and the latter, *an*, to *lan*; *an* is therefore the suffix of the first person plural, and *âp* is a conjunctive particle, like *û*, and is easily identified with Hebr. Chald. אַף 'also'; it occurs also in other inscriptions, but with other suffixes, e. g. *âpam* (Naksh-i Rajab, lin. 22. 24. Naksh-i Rustam, lin. 9.) 'I, also I', *âpash* (N. Raj. lin. 21. Pâî Kûlî, 10, lin. 3) 'he, also he, it'. In the two latter instances, we easily recognise the Pahlavî *âpam*, *âpash*, which the Parsis read *avam* and *avash* (see the index) [1]). The only difference between *âpan*

---

1) The reading *ajash* for does not require any further refutation, after finding the original form of the word in the inscriptions.

and *âpam*, or *âpash*, lies in the nature of the suffix; *am* and *ash* are Iranian, but *an* is clearly Semitic and expresses the first person plural; in the books we find used instead of *âpan*. In Chaldee the suffix of the first person plural is *ânâ*, but with the preposition לְ, it sometimes becomes לָן, in Syriac it is *an*, e. g. ܒܢ *ban*, 'in us', ܠܘܬܢ *l'votan*, 'at us, with us'.

Lin. 5. S. *âmat*, Ch. id., P. 'when, as'; see index, pag. 88.

S. *hatyâ*, Ch. *hararyâ*, P. *hatyâ*, 'an arrow'. That this is the meaning of *hatyâ*, follows unmistakeably from our glossary (10, 5.), in which it is explained by *tîr* تير 'an arrow'; it occurs five times in this inscription (lin. 5. 7. 8. 13. 15.) and is always rendered in Ch. by *hararyâ*, or *khararyâ* (חרריא), which must therefore mean the same. Both words are Semitic; *hatyâ*, or *khatyâ* is readily identified with Heb. Chald. חֵץ, Ethiop. *ḥess*, 'an arrow'; *t* = ט is frequently, in the Aramaic languages, the representative of Heb. צ, e. g. טְבַע = צְבַע 'to immerse', טוּר 'a mountain' = צוּר 'a rock'; *hararyâ*, or *khararyâ*, may be identified with Chald. גִּרְרָא, גִּירָא 'an arrow', as ח sometimes interchanges with ג, e. g. Heb. אֶפְרֹחַ = Syr. ܦܪܘܓܐ 'the young one of a bird'.

S. *shadîtun*, Ch. *shadît*, 'threw'. This is the verb belonging to *hatyâ*, and in lin. 8 *ramîtun* is used instead of it; the meaning of both verbs is 'to throw', which is another proof that *hatyâ* must mean 'arrow'. There are also passages in Pahlavî books, where *shadîtun* is used in connection with *tîr* which is, as we have seen, the equivalent of *hatyâ;* thus, in the Bundehesh 47, 1—2; 'they (the devils) throw (nails) at this bird like arrows'; Dîn-kart, vol. VII. pag. 282, lin. 5: 'the shooting of an arrow'. *Shadîtun*, *shadît*, are no doubt identical with Chald שְׁדָא, Syr. ܫܕܐ, 'to throw', which in both these languages, is chiefly used of the throwing of arrows; for instance, compare the Targum (Chaldee translation) of 1 Sam. 20, 3: גִּירָא דִּי שְׁדָא יְהוֹנָתָן 'the arrow which Jonathan threw'; 1 Sam. 20, 36: יַת גִּירַיָּא דַּאֲנָא שָׁדֵא 'the arrows which I threw (was throwing)': S. Ephræmi carmina Syriaca (ed. Hahn) 1, 3: ܘܐܣܟܠ ܫܕܐ ܓܐܪ̈ܐ ܠܠܠܝܐ 'who is foolish, throwing arrows at the nights' (i. e. one who seeks to unravel impenetrable mysteries); ibid. 17, 3 (pag. 129): ܐܘ ܫܕܐ ܓܐܪ̈ܐ ܠܛܘܪܐ ܪܒܐ ܠܐ ܬܬܚܡܢ ܕܓܐܪ̈ܝܟ ܡܩܒܠܝܢ. 'O (thou) who throwest (arrows) at a great mountain, do not believe thy arrows will hit'. Regarding the terminations *tun*, *t*, see section 4.

S. [illegible] *âdînan*, omitted in Ch., but in lin. 10 we have *âdîn* in both versions, 'then'; P. [illegible], אֱדַיִן (see index, pag. 90); *an* is the suffix of the first pers. plur. (comp. *âpan*). In the Pahlavî books it is used with the Iranian suffixes, as [illegible] *adînam* 'then by me', [illegible] *adînat* 'then by thee', in the Ardâî-Vîrâf-nâmeh; [illegible] *adînash* 'then by him', Bundehesh 4, 7. 59, 11. etc.; [illegible] *adînshân* 'then by them', Bund. 36, 15. 72, 16. etc.

S. [illegible] *lûînî* (*rûînî*), Ch. *qadmatman*, 'in the presence, before'; P. [illegible] = پيس (see index, pag. 198); it is best identified with Chald. לְעֵינַי 'in the eyes', i. e. before. There can be no doubt as to the meaning, as *qadmatman* must have the same signification, being connected with Chald. קְדָם, קֳדָם.

S. [illegible] *shataldalân, shatardarân*, Ch. *khshatardarîn*, 'satraps, governors'; this is an Iranian word whose primitive Persian form must have been *khshathra-dara*, 'holder of sway, ruler, governor', and equivalent to *khshathra-pâvâ*, 'satrap', in the Bisutun inscription.

Lin. 6. S. [illegible] *û barbîtân*, Ch. *barbîtân*; in Ch. *û*, Heb. Chald. וְ 'and', is omitted. This word occurs also, in its singular form [illegible], in the glossary (see index, pag. 94). It has been identified by Westergaard (Zend-avesta, vol I, preface, pag. 21, note 1) with Chald. בלבטין 'a councillor'; but this word, which occurs very rarely in Talmudic literature, seems to be only another orthography for בוליטין βουλευταί, 'senators' sing. בלווטים βουλευτής; and it appears strange for the Persians to have adopted a Greek word into Pahlavî, for a dignity, for which they might have used indigenous, or Semitic, terms; besides the words *bûlîtîn* and *barbîtân* do not correspond very closely in sound; I cannot therefore approve of this derivation. can be read *rabrabîtân*, instead of *û barbîtân*, but the corresponding *barbîtân* in Ch., and *barbîtâ* of the books, are opposed to this reading, as is also the recurrence of the conjunctive *û* before each of the other terms for dignities in S. lin. 6; however, if we assume the original Pahlavî pronunciation to have been *rebarbîtân*, which is quite possible, we can easily account for the dropping of the initial *r;* I therefore identify the word with Chald. רַבְרְבָן 'grandees, peers', Syr. ܪ̈ܘܪܒܢܐ; the first part *rab* is identical, the second *rabît* differs, and exhibits an abstract feminine formation; but such formations were used in the Semitic languages for denoting dignities held by men, as is shown by Heb. קֹהֶלֶת 'an orator before an assembly'.

S. (Wester.), Ch. *rabân.* The reading of this word in S. is doubtful, as Westergaard differs here from Stannus's plaster cast; the four last letters are clearly *lkân*, the first letter is apparently û. 'and', the second may be, but is very doubtful. According to Westergaard's copy, we should read *û ramanlakân*, a word which I cannot explain; it certainly signifies a class of noblemen, as it corresponds with Ch. *rabân* 'the great ones' (Heb. Chald. רַב 'great'); and the last four letters —*lkân* may suggest the reading *raûmalkân*, for *rabmalkân*. by which 'dukes, or counts', may perhaps be understood.

S. *û âzâtan*, Ch. *âzâtan*, 'noblemen'. This is probably the plural of the Persian آزاد 'a nobleman'; the omission of the long vowel *â* in the plural suffix, looks strange, but the same omission occurs in Ch. *yâztan* = S. *yaztân* pl. of *yazata*, in the sense of 'the supreme being'.

Lin. 6. 7. S. *âpan lagalman (ragalman) pavan zanman dîkî hanakhtûn*, Ch. *nagarîn pavîn (patan) zak vîm haqâîmût*, 'we placed the feet in this cave'. Of the meaning of this sentence there can be as little doubt, as of that of the preceding one, as the signification of the several words can be clearly made out. S. *lagalman*, Ch. *nagarîn*, (see also S. lin. 12) is P. لگد

ragalman, 'foot', Chald. רַגְלָא 'the foot'; *nagarîn* corresponds well with Chald. pl. רַגְלִין 'legs', the interchange of the liquid consonants being frequent in Pahlavî. S. *pavan* is P. 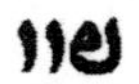 'in'; the corresponding word in Ch. may be read *pavîn*, or *patan*; whatever its etymology may be, its meaning is clear. S. *dîkî* is rendered in Ch. by *vîm*, both here and in lin. 13; the latter word is clearly Aryan, and is readily identified with the Zand *vaêma*, Vend. 4, 52. 13, 38. 15, 6. (Wester.) which must, according to the context, mean a 'ditch, hole, or pit', as a dog is mentioned as falling into something, a well, or water, or a ditch, etc.; regarding *dîkî* it is difficult to etymologize; the Persian دیگ *dêg*, which stands nearest, means 'a cooking pot, a cauldron', and the word occurs also in Pahlavî in this sense, as may be seen from the following passage from the Ardâî-Vîrâf-nâmeh: 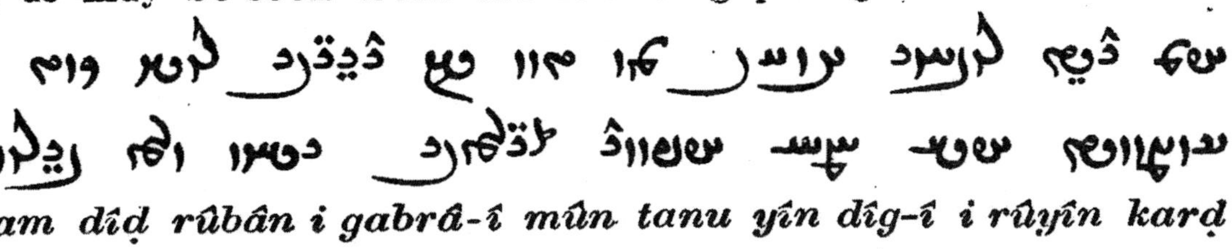 *apam dîḍ rûbân i gabrâ-î mûn tanu yîn dîg-î i rûyîn karḍ yekavîmûnêḍ, apash hamâî appunaḍ, lagalman-î i dashenu ulman bîrûnu i zak dîg yekavîmûnâḍ;* 'also by me was seen the soul of a man whose body was put into a brazen cauldron, also they always cook it; one foot that is the right, that shall remain outside of that cauldron'. As the inscription is at the entrance of a cave, it is only natural to understand *vîm* as 'cave', the rather as we obtain a perfectly clear sense by doing so. *Hanakhtûn* has been already identified by me, in the Zand-Pahlavi Glossary (pag. XXII.), with Chald. אַחֵת = אַנְחֵת 'to put down', from נְחַת 'to descend', 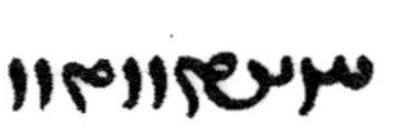 (index pag. 61); in Ch. it is rendered by *haqâîmût*, which I formerly read *hasâîmût*, but the character which was read *s*, appears to correspond to ק, as it is the initial letter of *qadmatman* in Ch. lin. 5; *haqâîmût* is clearly traceable to Heb. הֲקִימוּ, Chald. הֲקֵימוּ 'they placed', Hifil of קוּם 'to stand'; regarding the termination *t*, see remarks further on.

Lin. 7—8. S. 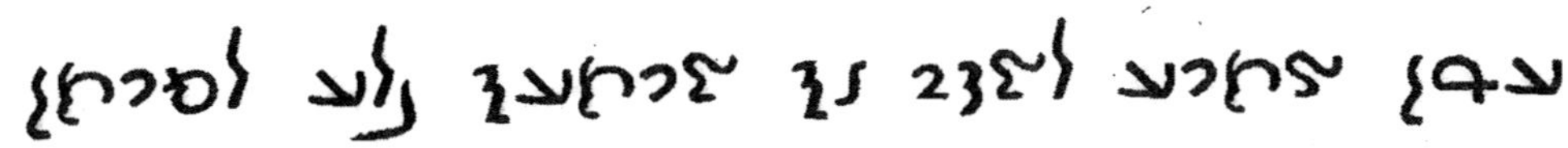
âpan hatyâ lachadu zak chîtâk barâ (balâ) ramîtun, Ch. *û hararyâ*

lahad (lakhad) lehû shîtî lebarâ ramît, 'we shot the arrow out (of the cave) that it might reach that target'. The meaning seems perfectly clear, though two words offer some difficulty, viz. *lachad* and *chîtâk*. The latter occurs also in lin. 9 and 15, and with the additional final *î*, forming *chîtâkî*, in lin. 11 and 14, and is always rendered in Ch. by *shîtî*. As the *chîtâk* is shot at, and is an object that has been built, or constructed, which follows from *banît*, 'built', in Ch. lin. 11, it must mean a kind of target constructed of wood, or earth, which was at some distance from the mouth of the cave. Etymologically, the word can only be traced to Sans. *chi*, 'to pile up, heap up, build up', which is chiefly used in the later Vedic books, with reference to the construction of a peculiar kind of altar, consisting of a large number of bricks; this is called *chayana* and *chiti; chitâ* is 'a pile of wood'. In the fragments of the Zand-avesta, which are still extant, the root *chi* does not occur in this sense; but that does not prove that it did not so exist in former times. In Pârsî and modern Persian, *chîdan* means 'to pick up, collect', thus in Mînôkhirad LXII. 41: *vash kâr iñ, ku ă thûm i ezh darakht i harvisp tukhma i Jaḍ-bēsh khasâneḍ, ôi chîneḍ, u ânô ku Tishtar âw staneḍ, frîneḍ*, 'and his (Chañmrôsh's) business is this, that he picks up that seed which has fallen off from the tree of all seeds, *Jaḍ-bēsh*, and carries it there where Tishtar keeps the water'. That *chi* had, in ancient Persian, the meaning 'to build, construct', follows clearly from the participle *chîtî* (comp. *kartî* in other inscriptions = [Pahlavi] *kartu*) in S. lin. 10. 12. corresponding with Ch. *banît*, which can only be traced to Chald. בְּנָה, Heb. בָּנָה 'to build'. S. *lachadû (lakhadû)*, Ch. *lahad*, is to be traced to Chald. אֲחַד 'to take, seize', here 'to hit'; the [Pahlavi] *ch*, in Westergaard's copy, is probably a misreading for [Pahlavi] *h, kh*, which always corresponds to the Ch. letter which is read *h, kh*, and occurs here in *lahad*, whereas [Pahlavi] *ch* always corresponds to the Ch. letter which is read *sh*. The form of the word is that of the infinitive, with the prefix לְ 'to, in order to'; not like the form used in Chaldee מֵיחַד, or Syriac ܡܐܚܕ, with the prefix *m*, but resembling the infinitive in Hebrew אֱחֹד, with לְ, לֶאֱחֹד, and in Assyrian (see **Menant** Grammaire Assyrienne, pag. 144. *ashab*, 'to inhabit'), in which languages the prefix *m* is not used in the infinitive. The *û*, in *lakhadû*, is the final ו *u* of the books, generally represented by [Pahlavi] *î* in the inscriptions; in Ch. it is wanting. S. *zak*, 'this', P. کو, is here rendered in Ch. by *lehû*, in lin. 13 by *hû* and in lin. 15 by *hûb*, while in Ch. lin. 14 we find *lehûp*; it is clearly the demonstrative pronoun הוּ = *zak*, with לְ, the characteristic of the dative, or accusative; *hû* stands in the same relationship to *hûb*, or *hûp*, as the Hebrew הוּא *hû* does to the Arabic هُوَ, which may have been pronounced *huva*, instead of *hûa* which is its modern pronunciation. S. *barâ*, P. بیرون, Ch. *lebarâ*, 'out, out of'; Chald. בָּרָא 'out, out of doors'. S. *ramîtun*, Ch. *ramît*, 'threw, shot'; Chald. רְמָא, Heb. רָמָה, Syr. ܪܡܳܐ, Arab. رَمَى, Ethiop. *ramaya*, 'to throw', often used of shooting arrows, like שְׁדָא; comp. the Targum of Jerem. 22, 7. הֵיךְ קַשְׁתָּא דְּרָמְיָא גִּרְרִין 'like a bow that shoots arrows'; Heb. Psalms 78, 9. רוֹמֵי קֶשֶׁת 'the shooters of bows', i. e. archers; Motanabbi carmina 158, 10. أَتَحْفُرُ عَلَى مَن رَمَتْهُ ٱللَّيَالُ 'dost thou protect him at whom the nights (i. e. misfortunes) shoot (arrows)'? The terminations *tun*, *t*, will be explained hereafter.

Lin. 8. S. [Pahlavi] [Pahlavi] [Pahlavi] *barâ ûlman vayâk*. Here the Ch. version seems to be wanting; after *lebarâ ramît*, corresponding to S. *barâ ramîtun*, there follows *bîsh* which has nothing corresponding in S. I connect *bîsh* with the verb *ramît*, and take it as the preposition בְּ, with the suffix of the 3[d] person singular, which as it is شَ in Persian and *shu* in Assyrian, may be traced either to a Semitic, or an Iranian source; *ramît bîsh* thus means 'we shot with it'; the occurence of the word *hararyâ*, 'arrow', in the same sentence, does not militate against this explanation of *bîsh*, for in the Semitic languages, the object can be expressed twice in the same sentence, once by a substantive and again by a pronoun. S. *ûlman* = P. [Pahlavi] 'that' (see the index, pag. 227.) [Pahlavi] *vayâk* can also be read *rayâk*, but it is difficult to make out its meaning, as no corresponding word can be discovered in Ch., where after *ramît bîsh*, there follows *tamman ânû hararyâ napalt lehavînd*, which I translate: 'there that arrow was falling down', i. e. it did not hit the target.

Which of these words expresses the meaning of *vayâk*, is not easily ascertained; *tamman*, 'there', occurs also in S. lin. 9, and is there followed by *vayâk*; *ânû* can be only a demonstrative pronoun, comp. Syr. ܗܢܘ, as the following *hararyâ*, 'arrow', seems to indicate; *napalt* may correspond, but this is a verb, and is readily identified with Chald. נְפַל 'to fall', and *lehavînd* which follows, serves only as an auxiliary verb to *napalt*, to express some tense, probably the imperfect, or perfect; it is used in the same way, but without the prefix *le*, in Ch. lin. 9—10: *yehût havîndî*, lin. 11—14: *kadab havînt*, and must no doubt be traced to Chald. הֲוָא; the grammatical nature of these forms will be considered hereafter. Returning to *vayâk*, although its meaning may correspond with *napalt*, it cannot be a verbal form, but seems to be a substantive, or adjective; we cannot trace it to the Semitic languages, and must therefore look for an Aryan etymology; we can derive it from the Zand root *vî* 'to go, move', whence *vayu* and *vaya*, not meaning 'air' as the element (as has been supposed by some scholars), but a certain genius who is always moving [1]); *vis*, pl. *vayô*, is 'bird' (Lat. *avis*), both in Zand and Vedic Sanscrit; in Vend. 5, 8. 9. *vayô* (nom. sing., to be distinguished from the pl. *vayô*, 'birds', in the same passage), Pâzand *vaê*, means an evil spirit who does injury to a man's life; but it may also mean a good genius, as may be seen from Mînokhirad II. 115 [2]), where the *vaê i veh*, i. e. the good genius, is connected with the angels Serosh and Behram, whilst the *vaê i vatar*, i. e. the evil genius, occurs in the same passage, associated with the devils. Although there can be little doubt as to the root of *vayâk*, it is impossible to determine its precise meaning, as neither 'bird', nor 'genius' will suit the sense of the context; it must express something indicative either of the flight of the arrow which had

---

1) *Vayu* and *vaya* should not be derived from *vâ* 'to blow', as has been done. The chief objection to such a derivation is that *â* does not generally become *a* in derivatives, comp. *vâta* 'wind', Sans. *vâyu*. The Zand *vayu* is therefore not identical with the Sans. *vâyu*.

2) I quote here from the MS. of E. W. West's edition of the Pâzand text, which will shortly be published with a translation and glossary.

been shot by the king, or of its having fallen to the ground, as is clearly stated in Ch. I propose taking it as an adjectival form, meaning 'moving, flying'; the verb 'to be' being understood; *barâ ûlman vayâk* thus means 'beyond it (the target), it was flying', i. e. it missed the target.

Lin. 8—9. S [Pahlavi script] *âîk hatyâ ramîtun tamman vayâk zak ârgûn lâ yahvûn,* 'whither the arrow had been shot, thither it was flying, (but) a place was not'. In Ch. there is no exact rendering of this passage, but its meaning is expressed by *tamman ânû hararyâ napalt lchavînd âtarman lâ yehût,* 'there that arrow was falling (but) a place was not (to receive it)'. S. *âîk* 'where, whither', is P. [Pahlavi script] *aîgh*, Chald. אֵיכָא 'where'; *tamman* is P. [Pahlavi script], Chald. תַּמָּן 'there'; *ârgûn* is difficult to explain, but as it is rendered in Ch. by *âtarman*, Chald. אֲתַר, אַתְרָא 'place', we are justified in assigning the same meaning to it; *lâ*, Ch. id., P. [Pahlavi script], Chald. לָא 'not'; *yahvûn* rendered by Ch. *yehût*, both here and in lin. 10, must be identified with P. [Pahlavi script] *yehevûntan*, Chald. הֲוָא 'to be' (see index, pag. 234); *lâ yahvûn* = *lâ yehût* = [Pahlavi script] 'it was not'; regarding the termination *t*, see hereafter.

Lin. 9—10. S. [Pahlavi script] *âîk hat chîtâk chîtî hûman âdîn bûlûnî (bîrûnî) patyâk yahvûn hûman;* Ch. *âîk âk shîtî banît havîndî kal lebarâ shaddarâ ârqî yehût havîndî.* The meaning of both texts must be the same, although Ch. contains more words than S.; the latter may be translated thus: 'where if a target had been constructed then it (the arrow) would have been visible outside'. S. *hat* is P. [Pahlavi script] 'if' (see the index, page 76); the corresponding Ch. *âk* is identical, in sound, with Heb. Chald. אַךְ 'only, certainly', but the latter is not used as a conditional particle, as *âk* is here. S. *chîtî hûman* is evidently a compound tense in the conditional mood, rendered in Ch. by *banît havîndî*, 'if it had been built'; the meaning of *chîtî* (past participle, with the final *î* instead of *û*) has been already explained; *hûman* occurs thrice in S., twice in lin. 10 and once in lin. 12, and is rendered in Ch. by *havîndî* in the first two places, and by *havînt* in the third. In the Pahlavî of the books, the conditional mood is expressed in the same manner, e. g. Vend. 1, 3. (Sp.): [Pahlavi] *hat li lâ yehabûnt hûmanaî*, 'if by me it had not been created'; this would be in the idiom of S.: [Pahlavi] *hat lî lâ yahbûn hûman;* the only difference being that the verbal terminations are wanting in S., but the [Pahlavi], or [Pahlavi] which is generally added to [Pahlavi] in this mood, though wanting in S., appears to be represented by *dî* in Ch. *havîndî*. As [Pahlavi] is also used in the formation of the past tense of the indicative, but with the Iranian personal terminations, and as these are wanting in S., *chîtî hûman* might have been taken as a past tense in the indicative mood, like *katab hûman*, 'wrote, has written', in S. lin. 12, but the particle *hat*, 'if', does not admit of this. *Havîndî* may be thus explained: *havîn*, or *hûîn*, is only another pronunciation for [Pahlavi] *hûman* = [Pahlavi], used as an auxiliary in the conjugation of the verb; *d* is the Iranian characteristic of the 3d person singular, and the final *î* indicates the conditional, as [Pahlavi] does in the Pahlavî of the books; when *havîn* is used for expressing the past tense in the indicative, only *t* is added, the *î* not being used, as in Ch. lin. 11: *yadâ kadab havînt*, 'a hand has written'. S. *âdîn* 'then', does not appear to be expressed in Ch., for the words *kal lebarâ* are evidently a translation of S. *bîlûnî*, Pers. بیرون 'outside' = the Semitic *lebarâ;* *kal*, in Ch. lin. 12. 13, represents S. [Pahlavi] *ûl* = Chald. עַל, and appears here in connection with *lebarâ*, as a kind of pleonasm; etymologically it is probably identical with עַל, if we take into consideration that ע, when sounded more harshly, would be pronounced something like *k*, or *kh*. S. *patyâk* seems to be expressed by Ch. *shaddarâ ârqî*, or by one of these words; both seem to be Semitic, but their meaning is difficult to ascertain; *shaddarâ* may be traced to Chald. שְׁדַר 'to send, discharge', (inf. Pael מְשַׁדְּרָא) which is frequently used (in Pael) with the duplication of the second radical; *ârqî* can only be identified with Chald אֲרַק, אַרְקָא (a harsher pronunciation for אַרְעָא = Heb. אֶרֶץ) 'earth'. If we take into consideration that targets are sometimes constructed against a mound of earth, the passage becomes intelligible, and thus the words: *âk shîtî.... ârqî yehût havîndî,* will mean: 'if a target had been built, there would have been (sufficient) earth to discharge (the arrow at) outside (that it might stick there)'. As regards S. *patyâk,* it may be connected with P. *paitâk*, Pers. پیدا 'evident, manifest'; and the whole passage thus means: if a target had been constructed, at the place where the arrow had struck.

Lin. 11—12. S. *âkhar lanman parmât minû chîtâkî âûlandalî chîtî;* Ch. *âdîn lan âûpdasht minû shîtî panman qatar banît âvat.* All the words in S., except *âûlandalî* are easily intelligible; *akhâr* is P. Heb. אחר 'afterwards', and is rendered in Ch. by *âdîn* which we also found in S. lin. 5; *lanman* is P. 'we' (see the index, pag. 198), and in Ch. we have *lan*, Chald. לָן, (comp. Ch. lin. 5, and the note on *âpan* S. lin. 4). S. *parmât*, P. , Pers. فرموده 'ordered'; Ch. *âûpdasht* is of Aryan origin, and is evidently a past participle, the original form of which appears to have been *upadishta*, from Zand *dis*, 'to show, instruct', + *upa;* its meaning is the same as that of *parmât*, 'ordered'; the initial *â* = א, in *âûp*, is probably only a *mater lectionis* for introducing the vowel *û*, according to the Semitic system of writing which has been adopted in Pahlavî. S. *minû chîtâkî*, Ch. *minû shîtî*, 'an invisible target'; for the meaning of *minû*, see lin. 2; the *î* in *chîtâkî*, both here and in S. lin. 14, is not the *idhâfet*, but the final vowel, like *î* in *bagî*, which is expressed in the Pahlavî of the books by *u*. S. *âûlandalî* is just as unintelligible to me, as its corresponding Ch. *panman qatar;* it may probably be divided into two words, *âûlan* and *dalî*, and may also be read *âvaran-darî; âûlan* = *âvaran* may be connected with P. *avânîk* (*avârîk*, index, pag. 81) 'the rest, the others'; it would then correspond to Zand *aora* = Sans. *avara*, 'lower, following, later', Pâz. *awarē; darî* could be traced to *dare, dere* = Sans. *dhṛi*, 'to hold'; the whole would be a compound and mean 'holding for the future generations', i. e. which would be respected by people in future. Ch. *panman* may be connected wiih Heb. פָּנִים, לִפְנֵי 'before'; instead of *qatar*, perhaps *satar* may be read, as E. W. West does, who identifies it with Heb. סְתַר 'an enclosure, a hiding-place'; but the explanation is in every way difficult, and I leave it to future investigators. After Ch. *bànît*, 'built', which is the translation of S. *chîtî*, there follows a word which I read *âvat* אות, but which is not expressed in S.; it may be taken as a particle, meaning 'then', but I cannot find corresponding words in the Semitic languages; I connect it with *banît*, and take it as an auxiliary verb, derived from הֲוָא 'to be'; the change from ה to א not offering any great difficulty.

Lin. 12. S. [illegible] *minû yadman katab kûman*; Ch. *minû yadâ kadab havînt*; 'an invisible hand wrote'. S. *yadman*, Ch. *yadâ*, is P. [illegible] 'hand' (see the index, pag. 234.) S. [illegible] both here and in lin. 16, can hardly be read otherwise than *katab*, as it is represented, in both places, by Ch. *kadab* כדב which can be identified only with Heb. Chald. כתב 'to write'; [illegible] must therefore be taken as a compound character, equivalent to [illegible]; *hûman* forms the past tense. In the Pahlavî of the books, the sentence would run: [illegible].

Lin. 12—13. S. [illegible] *zak lagalman* (*ragalman*) *pavan zanman dîkî âyû hanakhtûn*, Ch. *nagarîn pavîn zanman vîm hîp haqâîmûd*, 'do not put the feet in this cave', i. e. do not take a stand here. All the words of this sentence, in both texts, have been already explained, except S. *âîû*, or *âyû*, and the corresponding Ch. *hîp*; this word occurs also in S. lin. 14, and in both places it precedes the verb, where the sense requires a prohibitive particle; on closer investigation it is not difficult to explain *âyû* and *hîp* as prohibitive particles from the Semitic languages; comp. Heb. אַיִן 'it is not, it was not', sometimes shortened to אִי, e. g. אִי־נָקִי 'the innocent', Job. 22, 30.; which shortening is of frequent occurrence in the language of the Mishna [1]); in Ehiopic אַי *'î* is prefixed to both nouns and verbs to denote the general negation, and may also be used as a prohibitive, e. g. *'ît'qetlu nafsô* 'do not kill him', Gen. 37, 21. [2]); in the same prohibitive sense, the particle *ai* occurs also in the Assyrian, e. g. *ai ipparkû* 'they shall not be broken' [3]). The only difference between S. *âyû*, Ch. *hîp*, and the Semitic אַי is that the two former have a final *û*, or *p*, which is wanting in the latter. Regarding the final *p* in *hîp* (where *h* = א), it is to be observed that the Ch. version employs this letter also after *û* in *kal hûp* (lin. 13), and *lehûp* (lin. 14), where it appears to be a *v*, or *w*, pronounced after *û*. The only way in which the final *û* can be explained, is by taking it as the *u* of the original nominative, the final ۏ *u* which we find so frequently in Pahlavi, as also in Assyrian and Arabic; this is not surprising, as the particle was regarded as a noun, as is clearly shown by the Arabic أَيُّمَن 'every one', the first part of which, *'ayyu*, is identical with אַי, though its meaning is originally interrogative, but the close connection between the interrogative pronoun and the negative particle is well known. Ch. *haqâîmûd* is the same as *haqâîmût* in Ch. lin. 7, *d* and *t* being interchangeable at the end of words, as they are in the Pahlavî of the books; with regard to this termination see section 4.

Lin. 13—14. S. 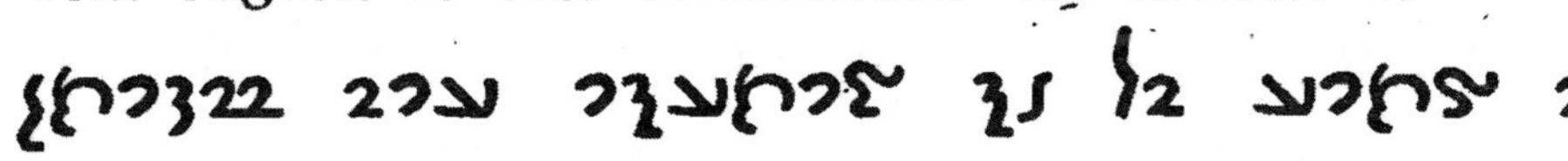
û hatyâ·ûl zak chîtâkî âyû shadîtun, Ch. *û hararyâ kal hû shîtî hîp shadyû*, 'and do not shoot arrows at that target'. All the words in this sentence have been already explained; but with regard to the form of *shadyû*, it is the 3d pers. pl. שַׁדִּיו, of the so-called perfect (first tense) in Chald. of the Pael שַׁדָּא 'to throw, shoot'; the Iranian termination being here omitted.

Lin. 14—15. S. 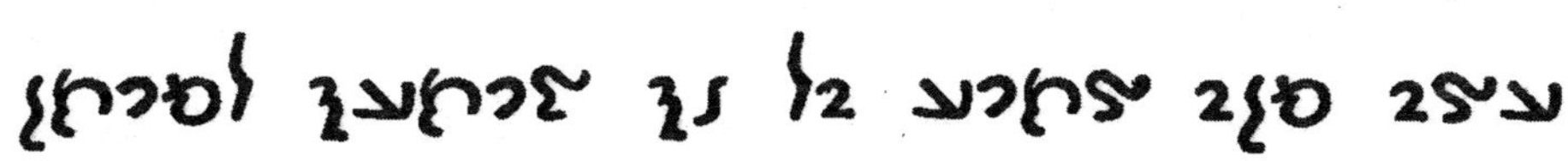
âkhar minû hatyâ ûl zak chîtâk ramîtun, 'after an invisible arrow has

1) See Ewald, Lehrbuch der hebräischen Sprache, pag. 476 (6th edition).
2) See Dillmann, Grammatik der äthiopischen Sprache, pag. 398.
3) See Norris, Assyrian Dictionary, vol. I. pag. 3.

been shot at this target'; Ch. *minû hararyâ kal hûp shîtî yâmzûd.* The Ch. version does not here quite agree with S., the particle *âhhar*, 'after', being omitted; as *yâmzûd* corresponds to *ramîtun*, it must of course express a similar idea; it can only be taken as the 3ᵈ pers. pl. of the imperfect (second tense) of the Hifil of Heb. מָצָא. Chald. מְטָא 'to come, to arrive', which in Chaldee is יְמַטּוּן; here it means: 'they have made an invisible arrow (or arrows) arrive at that target, i. e. hit it'.

Lin. 16. S. 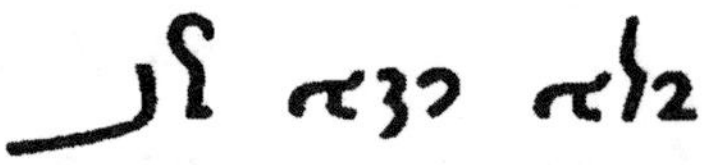 *ûlman yadman katab*, Ch. *lehûp yadâ havîndî*, 'such wrote the hand'. S. *ûlman* = P.  'this, that, such' (see the index, pag. 227); it is rendered by Ch. *lehûp*; *le* = לְ, being in Chaldee the sign of the accusative, as well as of the dative, see also Ch. lin. 7. *hûp* is *hû* הוּא 'he, that, it'.

Having thus given a full commentary on both texts of the inscription, I propose the following translation of S.:

'This is the edict of me, the Ormazd-worshipper, the divine being Sapor, the king of kings of Irân and non-Irân, of heavenly origin from God; the son of the Ormazd-worshipper, the divine being Ardeshîr, the king of kings of Irân, of heavenly origin from God; the grandson of the divine being Bâbek, the king. As we shot this arrow, then we shot it in the presence of the satraps, the grandees, peers and noblemen; we put the foot in this cave; we threw the arrow outside that it should reach that target; the arrow (was) flying beyond that (target); whither the arrow had been thrown, there was no place (to hit), where if a target had been constructed, then it (the arrow) would have been manifest (?). Afterwards it was ordered by us: 'an invisible target is constructed for the future (?); an invisible hand has written: 'do not put the foot in this cave, and do not shoot an arrow at this target, after an invisible arrow has been thrown at this target'; such wrote the hand'.

The Ch. version contains some deviations, which have been discussed in the commentary. The general tenor of the inscription is easily intelligible. The king Sapor, surrounded by his grandees and noblemen, took his stand in the cave, on the wall of which this inscription is found, to shoot an arrow at a target which was at some distance from the mouth of the cave; the arrow missed the target, and fell to the ground, as clearly appears from Ch. lin. 8: 'there that arrow fell'. That the king's arrow did not hit the mark, was perhaps regarded as auguring evil for him and his rule, and he could not acknowledge that he had met with such a disaster; hence the fiction of an invisible target, an invisible hand, and an invisible arrow, things which are quite in accordance with Zoroastrian ideas (see above, pag. 50). It was then supposed that at the spot where the arrow fell, after missing its mark, there was an invisible target to receive the invisible counterpart of the visible arrow; hence it is expressly stated that 'if at that place where the arrow was flying, a target had been constructed, the arrow would have hit it, in a manner visible to all lookers-on'. The event was made a kind of miracle by the further fiction, that an invisible hand had written (probably on the wall of the cave, on one of those tablets which have been left blank) that: nobody should enter this cave, or shoot arrows at a certain target. No doubt a target was afterwards constructed on the spot where the arrow had fallen to the ground, in commemoration of the event. On what occasion the king shot the arrow, and for what purpose, we cannot ascertain; it was probably some symbolical act, the arrow being supposed to be directed at some enemy who was to be pierced in a mystical way.

b) The Naksh-i Rajab inscription.

This inscription, which comprises 31 lines, is one of the longest, and perhaps the best preserved of all the inscriptions. Judging from what may be read with some degree of certainty, its contents appear to be of a religious character. The sculptures close to it, represent the king receiving, from Ormazd, a chaplet which appears to be the symbol of empire, possibly a crown. In the inscription itself there frequently occurs the word [Pahlavi] *kartîr* (lin. 1. 22. 23. 27. 29. 30. 31.) which may refer to this chaplet, or crown; Thomas and West identify it with the Heb. כֶּתֶר 'crown', the *cidaris* of the Persian kings; and I cannot propose any better explanation. The form *kartîr* does not offer much difficulty, if we start from the Hebrew Piel, or Chaldee Pael, (intensive form) in which the root כתר 'to surround', is chiefly used, and not in Qal (the unmodified active verb); *kartîr* then stands for *kattîr*, the *r* taking the place of the duplication of the medial consonant, as is frequently the case in Chaldee, in the formation of the so-called quadriliterals. The date of this inscription is later than that of the Hâjîâbâd inscriptions, as towards the end of it, there are several names of kings mentioned, Shahpûhrî (Shâpûr), Aûharmazdî (Ormazd), and two Varahrân (Behrâm), whence we are justified in concluding that it is not older than the time of Behrâm II. (A. D. 274—291).

As we possess only one complete transcript [1]) of this inscription, in which the letters are often much distorted, and which is not sufficiently accurate to admit of a transliteration and translation of the whole, I shall confine myself here to the explanation of some words and phrases which seem to be readily intelligible. It is true that E. Thomas has furnished us with a complete transliteration of the inscription in Persian characters [2]), but though valuable as a first attempt, it would be impossible to make an intelligible translation from it; indeed taking into consideration the evident inaccuracy of Flandin's transcript, any complete transliteration from it could not be otherwise than full of hazardous guesses, which cannot be substantiated by philological interpretation. E. W. West has treated the inscription with more caution [3]); he pointed out merely those words and sentences which he thought might be read with some degree of certainty, and only ventured upon a tentative translation of the whole of the last six lines (26—31). Several words and phrases have also been explained by me, in my article 'on the character of the Pahlavî language, with

1) Flandin, Voyage en Perse, vol. IV. plate 190.

2) Early Sassanian Inscriptions, seals and coins, pag. 34—37.

3) Sassanian inscriptions explained by the Pahlavî of the Pârsîs, pag, 27—30, of the separate impression (Journal of the R. As. Soc. new-series vol. IV.)

special reference to the Sasanian inscriptions [1]), but I did not venture to go as far as my friend has done; I shall now repeat these explanations, with some additions.

Lin. 2. *vazlûnî*, P. *vazlûntan* (see the index, pag. 230) 'to go'; the same word, but in the form *vazlûnt*, occurs in lin. 19, and also in Naksh-i Rûstam lin. 14; *vazlûnî* would be in the 2ᵈ person, but I think it must be read *vazlûnt* (in the 3ᵈ person), as I cannot well imagine how the 2ᵈ person could be applied in the beginning of the inscription.

Lin. 4—5. *vahîshtî û dûshkhûî*, 'paradise and hell'; the same terms occur also in lin. 8. and 17—18, so there can be no doubt regarding the reading.

Lin. 6. Here the following words are clear: = *maman*, 'which, what', = , = *yehevûn* (*yahvûn*), 'it is, exists'.

Lin. 10—11. *û ratî yahvûn hûmanam û pavan nafshman* = . Although these words are very legible, and easily intelligible, I cannot venture on translating the whole sentence to which they belong, as the preceding and following words cannot be recognised; *ratî* is the Zand *ratu* 'chief, head', and *ratî yahvûn hûmanam* is 'I have been the head'; *û pavan nafshman* is 'and for myself, as regards myself'; for *nafshman* see the index, pag. 164.

Lin. 11—12. *yahvûn hûmanam û madam zanman* (*va*)*hîshtî* = 'I have been, and on this paradise'. In the text there is only *hîshtî*, but as the word *vahîshtî* frequently occurs in this inscription, I think that the initial *va* has been omitted by the transcriber. The

---

1) Sitzungsberichte der Kgl. baierischen Akademie der Wissenschaften, for Feb. 1869, pag. 9 of the separate impression.

words which precede *yahvûn hûmanam*, may be read […] *lî taltûî*, and the meaning would be 'I have been the third; this appears to be confirmed by lin. 12—13: […] *shatlîtî lî terê yahvûnt*, 'I possessed two rules (ruling powers)'; *terê* is evidently […] 'two', […] representing *r*.

Lin. 13. […] *lî yahvûn hûmanam* = […] 'I have been'. […] *û min yâzdân âmak (hamak) yahmalunt*, 'and all have come from God'. The most illegible word in the sentence is *yâzdân*, but I doubt if the characters can be read otherwise; the […] *â* in the first syllable is no great difficulty, as the word is written *yâztan* in the Ch. version of the Hâjîâbâd inscription. The […] in […] is distorted in Flandin's transcript, but there can be little doubt about the correctness of my reading, as we find the same word very clearly written with […] in lin. 21. The whole sentence would run thus, in the Pahlavî of the books: […] *û men yazdân hamak yahmtûnt (jâmtûnt)*.

Lin. 14. […] *zak pavan yazdân yamashkhûn*. The first three words are well known from the Pahlavî texts; but the last, *yamashkhûn* which is a verb (3d pers. sing.), is not mentioned in the list of verbs in the Pahlavî-Pâzand Glossary, nor have I met with it in any Pahlavî book, so far as I am aware; there can be no doubt as to the correctness of the reading, as the word occurs again in lin. 23. Its meaning can only be guessed at, as the Chald. מְשַׁח I. 'to measure', II. 'to anoint', is not applicable to the sense of either of the passages; it appears to mean 'to obtain, receive', and I suppose it is a corruption of a quadriliteral verb (comp. Syr. ܡܣܟܶܢ 'to impoverish'), the full form of which may have been *mashkakh*, in which case it might be traced to Chald. שְׁכַח, Afel אַשְׁכַּח 'to find, obtain' (comp. *ashkahônatan* in the index, pag. 73). The whole sentence I translate by: 'he obtains (obtained) this through God'.

Lin. 14—15. […]

û tamman lûbân (*rûbân*) *lâtî* (*râtî*) *û lâstî* (*râstî*) *âyû yahvûn*, 'and there shall not be the soul of the liberal and righteous (man)'. The sense is clear, and all the words occur also in the Pahlavî of the books, except *âyû*, regarding which see pag. 62. [Pahlavi] *û madam* can be clearly read in lin. 15, as it has been also in lin. 12.

Lin. 18—19. [Pahlavi] [Pahlavi] [Pahlavi] *vahîshtî âitî û dûskhûî* = [Pahlavi] [Pahlavi] [Pahlavi] 'there is a paradise and a hell'. [Pahlavi] *aîti yemanûn kalît lî û daglâkh ûl vahîshti vazlûnt minû bachak lî zak ûl dûshkhûî ramîtun*, 'some one says: I have read that the pious (works) go to heaven (but) my spiritual sins are thrown into hell'. There can be hardly any doubt of the general meaning of this sentence; the word which I have read *yemanûn*, is not very legible in Flandin's copy, where the first three letters [Pahlavi] *y m n* are clear enough, but the last two are much distorted, though they can hardly represent anything but [Pahlavi] *ûn*, especially as the phrase [Pahlavi] [Pahlavi] *âît yemanûnad*, 'some one says', is very frequently used in the Pahlavî books. *Kalît lî* would be, in common Pahlavî, [Pahlavi] [Pahlavi] *kerîtûnt le*, 'I have read, or called', comp. Chald. קְרָא; the termination *ûn*, *ûnt*, which is usually added to the Semitic verbs, in Sasanian Pahlavî, is here omitted, as it is in Chaldæo-Pahlavî (comp. *shadît* for *shadîtun*). *Daglâkh* can only be traced to the Zand *dañgra*, 'pious, virtuous', and must refer to works, as appears from the following sentences; *bachak* is Pers. بزه 'crime, sin'.

Lin. 19—20. [Pahlavi] *û minû kalp kalt hûman û madam kalp kalt bar sazîtunt*, 'and (if) the spiritual (good) works have been done, and the fruit for the work done goes forth'. *Kalp* (*karp*) is the well known Pahlavî word [Pahlavi] *karfak* کرفه; the final *ak* is here omitted, which may be a mistake of the copyist; as the following word *kart* begins with the same letter *ka*, and he may have written it once, instead of twice. The last letter of *madam* is indistinct, but it can hardly be anything but ס, especially as the preposition *madam* is wanted to complete the sense; *bar* is Pers. بر 'fruit'; *sazîtûnt* is the [Pahlavi] *sazîtûntan*, 'to go', of the books, see the index, pag. 206.

Lin. 20—21. בעכיסתן כדן כיסתונין עגמון זלה עכתונין

û âîmat yadman yahmatûnt âpash ûlman âstûndî, 'and whatever hand came forth, he saw it'. The last letter of כדן is indistinct, looking like ג, but there exists no such word as *yadap; âîmat* is [Pahlavi] 'which, how', generally read *admat*; *yahmatûnt*, 'he came', is identical with [Pahlavi], see the index, pag. 133; *âpash* with [Pahlavi], as before explained; *ûlman*, 'it, him', with [Pahlavi], see the index, pag. 227; *âstûndî*, 'he saw', with [Pahlavi] *âstûntu*.

Lin. 21—22. סנס כיסתונין כיסתונ לי זכרתו כיסתונ עגס נזן עמסנ לי עסנתגס עגמונ *minam yahmatûnt chîgûn lî kartîr yahmatûn âpam zanman nâmak ûl khâchalân (khshatardarân?) nipishtî*, 'from me it came; how the crown has come to me, (on this event) I have written this letter to the satraps'. The most illegible word is *khâchalân*, which can be only a corruption of some better known word, I suspect *khshatardarân;* the second character can also be read גג, in which case the word begins with *khsh.* All the words, except *kartîr* (before explained), occur in the Pahlavi of the books; *chîgûn*, 'how', is [Pahlavi]; *nâmak* is نامه 'book, letter'; *nipishtî* is نپشت 'written'.

Lin. 22—23. עכן סט לי זכרתו סנן נז עזנזני סן גגתלדרן יכסגגגס *âîk maman lî kartîr manak zî âvzûnî min shataldarân yamashkhûn*, 'that as regards me, I received a diadem as a symbol (?) of increase (increasing power) from the satraps'. Although the characters are legible enough, the translation of the passage is difficult; *maman lî*, 'concerning me', i. e. I; *manak* may be traced to *man* 'to think', here it appears to mean a token of remembrance, or a symbol;

avzûnî is Pers. افزونی 'increase', and is well known from the Pahlavî books; the verbal form *afzût*, 'may he grow, or increase', is used on coins (see pag. 8); regarding *yamashkhûn*, see pag. 68.

Lin. 24. *pâtakhshatlî hatîmûd âpam dabîr nafshman.* The sentences are incomplete, as neither the preceding, nor the following, words are legible in the transcript. *Pâtakhshatlî* is the modern Persian پادشاهی 'supreme rule'; the same word occurs also in lin. 25 and 26, and frequently in the Naksh-i Rûstam inscription 1), lin. 12. 18. 32, and in lin. 5. 7. in the form *pâtakhshatrî;* it is there often found with the verb *hatîmûd*, as it is here; *hatîmûd* is *âtîmûntan* (see index, pag. 76) which is explained by *anbēshtan, anbâshtan*, 'to fill'. In the index I compared it with Heb. אָטַם 'to stop, shut', before I knew of its occurrence in the inscriptions; as its initial letter is *h*, or *kh*, in all the four passages in which it is found, lin. 24. *hatîmûd*, Naksh-i Rustam lin. 5. *hatîmûn*, 18. *hatîmûnd*, and 32. *hatîmûnt*, (which forms represent the 3d pers. sing. of the present tense, or the past participle) the derivation proposed in the index cannot be correct, nor would it give any adequate sense; the word must be a Hifil of the root תָּמַם 'to be complete', which in Hebrew is הֵתַם 'to complete, to finish'; in the infinitive a suffix is joined to it, and there even occurs the form הָתִים (Isaiah 33, 1. כַּהֲתִימְךָ 'on thy finishing') which exactly agrees with *hatîmûn*; in connection with *pâtakhshatrî*, it must mean 'the supreme power is made complete', i. e. it has been obtained. The next word *âpam* is 'I', being composed of *âp* + *m*, see above pag. 51; *dabîr* is Pers. دبیر 'a writer'; *nafshman* is (see index, pag. 164.)

Lin. 25. *pâtakhshatlî û mâtân yektîbûn;* so the characters read. *Pâtakhshatlî* is already explained; *yektîbûn* is , Chald. כְּתַב 'to write'; *û*, or *r*, be-

1) See Flandin, Voyage en Perse, vol. IV. pl. 181.

fore *mâtân* cannot be explained, and is probably a mistake, as 'and' is not suited to the meaning of the passage; the correct reading is suggested by lin. 26, where [Pahlavi] *pâtakhshatlî* is followed by the word [Pahlavi] *mâtîkân* (Flandin's transcript gives [Pahlavi] instead of [Pahlavi], but these two letters are frequently confounded by him) which is [Pahlavi] *mâdîgân*, 'history, tale' (see the index, pag. 157). If we read *pâtakhshatlî mâtîkân yektîbûn*, we can translate it by 'he writes the history of the empire (or emperor)'.

Lin. 26—27. [Pahlavi] *âkharaz nâmakî khazîtunt âîk yekarîtunt âîk ânmanach kartî(r) hûmanam*, 'after he had seen the letter, he then exclaimed, 'I have done this'; *âkhar* is [Pahlavi] 'after'; *khazîtunt* is [Pahlavi] 'to see'; *yekarîtunt* (in Flandin's transcript there is again [Pahlavi] instead of [Pahlavi]) is evidently [Pahlavi] *karîtûntan*, 'to call, read'; the initial *y* is remarkable, as this word is generally used in Pahlavî without this prefix. The meaning of *ânmanach* is not clear; it appears to be a demonstrative pronoun, comp. Syr. [Syriac], *ânû* in Chaldæo-Pahlavî; *ach* being the Pahlavî suffix [Pahlavi] 'also' but often used merely to emphasize the word to which it is added. Instead of *kartîr*, we should read *kartî*.

Lin. 27—28. [Pahlavi] *Shahpûhrî malkân malkâ kartîram magûpat û âîharpat Rûm kaltî hûmanam.* It is not easy to ascertain the general sense of this passage, although there is little difficulty in reading the transcript, and we know most of the words, which are also repeated in the two following sentences; but the interpretation of the two words [Pahlavi] and [Pahlavi], or [Pahlavi], is perplexing. If the transcript be correct, the first of these may be read *kîtrûm*, *kîtûram*, or *kîtsham*, but I should be at a loss to etymologize any of these readings, and an emendation is necessary for obtaining an intelligible translation. The simplest change is to read *kartîram*, as *kartîr* occurs frequently in the inscription, and ט *m* is the pronominal suffix of the 1st person singular. In lin. 29. *kartîr* is followed by *zî Aûharmazdî*, in lin. 30. by *zî bûkht-lûbân Varahrân û Aûharmazdî*, and in lin. 31. by *zîam Shah*..; it is thus twice followed by names of kings (first by Hormazd and then by Behrâm and Hormazd), once by the pronoun 'my', and once by the same with the name of Shahpûhrî. As Hormazd and Behrâm are called (lin. 29) *Shahpûhrkan*, i. e. descendants of Shahpûhr (Shâpûr, or Sapor), the Shahpûhr who is mentioned in lin. 27, must be their predecessor, and the Varahrân who (in lin. 30) is called *Varahrânkan*, i. e. son of Behrâm, must be the second Behrâm, and his is the latest royal name which occurs here. Thus the kings from Shâpûr I. to Behrâm II. are mentioned in their regular succession, viz. Shâpûr I. A. D. 238 — 269, Hormazd I. 269 — 271, Behrâm I. 271 — 274 and Behrâm II. 274 — 291. The word *kartîram* is followed by *magûpat û âîharpat Rûm*, but in lin. 29 and 30, there is only *magûpat Rûm* after the royal name; *âîharpat* is clearly [Pahlavi] 'herbad', Z. *aêthrapaiti*, and occurs also in the Pâî Kûlî inscription 2, 1, and in that of Naksh-i Rustam lin. 8; *magûpat* is [Pahlavi] 'mobed', it occurs thrice here and also in N. R. lin. 33. These words are always followed here by טגג *Rûm*, or טגג *sham*; it is difficult to decide which reading is correct; if we read *sham*, 'name', it means, in connection with the following *kaltî hûmanam*, 'I have made a name', i. e. I have called, but in this case the name of the king should be in the dative case; the dative particle however does not occur, and therefore this interpretation is doubtful. If we read *Rûm*, the meaning would be: I have made such and such a king mobed of *Rûm*; but can this statement be accounted for? It might refer to the victory of Shâpûr I. over the Roman emperor Valerian, who was made prisoner by the Persian king; and as the Roman emperor was Pontifex Maximus, it is not impossible that Shâpûr may have assumed this title of the vanquished emperor, which was afterwards inherited by his successors, Hormazd and the two Behrâms. There remains still one difficulty, viz. the word *kartîram*. As I take *kartîr* as 'crown' (see pag. 65), the whole sentence may be thus translated: 'I have made Shâpûr the king of kings, my crown, the high-priest of Rûm'. The speaker is no doubt Ahura-mazda who is presenting the *cidaris* to king Shâpûr; 'my crown' must mean 'my representative, sovereign in my stead'. God himself had invested him with sovereign power, not only over Persia, but even over Rome whose emperor he had vanquished. This sovereignty was inherited by his successors, Hormazd and the two Behrâms; hence the crown is called, in the following lines, no longer 'my crown', but 'the crown of Hormazd', or that 'of Behrâm'.

Lin. 28—29. [illegible] *û Aûharmazdî malkân malkâ û Valahlân malkân malkâ zî Shahpûhrkan kartîr zî Aûharmazdî magûpat Rûm kaltî hûmanam*; 'I made Hormazd king of kings, and Behrâm king of kings, the descendants of Shâpûr, (and) the crown of Hormazd, high-priest of Rûm'. The word *zî* occurs frequently in the inscriptions (see lin. 23. 27. 30. Pâî Kûlî 1, 3. 3, 2. 8, 3. 19, 2. 3. 4. Naksh-i Rustam lin. 4. 8. 10. 17. 31. etc.) and is the relative pronoun corresponding to کی in the books. *Shahpûhrkan* can hardly express any thing else but descendant of Shâpûr, though the form ought to be *Shahpûhrân*.

Lin. 29—31. [illegible] *û Valahlân malkân .... zî Valahlânah kartîr zî bûkht-lûbân Valahlân û Aûharmazdî magûpat Rûm kaltî hûmanam*; 'I have made Behrâm (king of) kings, the son of Behrâm, (and) the crown of the deceased Behrâm and Hormazd, high-priest of Rûm'. *Valahlânah* stands probably for *Valahlânakan*, or *Valahlânân*; comp. *Shahpûhrkan*. The expression *bûkht-lûbân* (*rûbân*) occurs also in N. R. lin. 33; it corresponds, in meaning, to the [illegible] *anûshak-rûbân* of the books, an epithet which is applied to a deceased person, and means 'one whose soul is safe, or without injury'; *bûkht* means 'purified, liberated', comp. Pâzand *bôkhtan*, 'to purify', Z. *buj*, 'to clean, purify'.

Lin. 31. is too much mutilated to admit of translation; the words

 *nipishtî* and 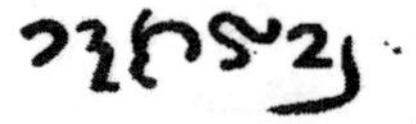 *bûkhtakî* are legible enough; the former means 'written', or 'writing'; the latter is the abstract of *bûkht*, and may mean 'purification, liberation'; the following word may be read 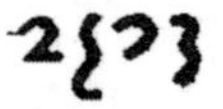 *dinû* = دين 'religion', but this is not certain.

c) The remaining Pahlavî inscriptions.

The Hâjîâbâd and Naksh-i Rajab inscriptions are the most important of all those which are extant, for philological purposes, as they are of some length and well preserved. It is true, the Naksh-i Rustam and Pâi-Kûlî inscriptions are more extensive, but we know them only in such a mutilated and fragmentary form, that it is hardly possible to venture upon the translation of a whole sentence. While the remaining inscriptions are too short to be now of much interest, as they contain nothing but names and titles which are already known. I shall therefore confine myself here to remarks upon such words in the longer inscriptions, as can be read with some degree of certainty; some of them have been already quoted, as collateral proofs, in the explanation of the preceding inscription.

The longest of all the known Pahlavî inscriptions, appears to be that of Naksh-i Rustam which comprises 70 lines, none of them, however, complete [1]). It is illustrated by a bas-relief [2]) representing the king crowned and on horseback, holding one of his enemies bound and standing at his horse's head, while another is on one knee in a suppliant attitude; behind the horse is the inscription, and above it appear the head and shoulders of an attendant, with arm and fore-finger uplifted, as if calling attention, and standing as it were behind a wall on which the writing is inscribed; he may be a scribe, and the prisoners are probably Romans.

The date of the inscription cannot be exactly ascertained. Three names occur with the royal title, viz. *Shahpûhrî* (lin. 1. 2. 6.), *Aûhar-*

---

1) See Flandin, Voyage en Perse, vol. IV. pl. 181 and 181-bis.
2) Ibid. pl. 185.

mazdî (lin. 9) and *Valahlân* (lin. 40), who apparently represent the second, third and fourth kings of the Sasanian dynasty. As *Valahlân* = Behrâm is also mentioned in lin. 33, though without a legible title, but with the epithet *bûkht-lûbân*, i. e. deceased (see pag. 74), we may conclude that the inscription is later than the reign of Behrâm I., and may date from the end of the 3^d century A. D., like the Naksh-i Rajab inscription. Both are alike in style, and show a rather marked difference from the Sasanian version of the Hâjiâbâd inscription, as they use the Iranian verbal terminations *m* and *t*, which are wanting in the latter.

Lin. 1. 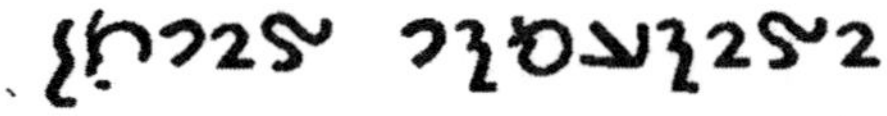 *û hû-kâmakî havîtan (havîtun)*; *hû-kâmakî* is evidently 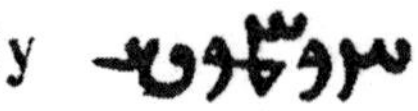 'good desire'; *havîtun* (here and in lin. 2) is from the same root as *yahvûn*, viz. הֲוָא 'to be'; it should probably be read *havîtun* (comp. *shadîtun*) and is formed in the same way as other verbs derived from Semitic roots in ל״ה.

Lin. 2. 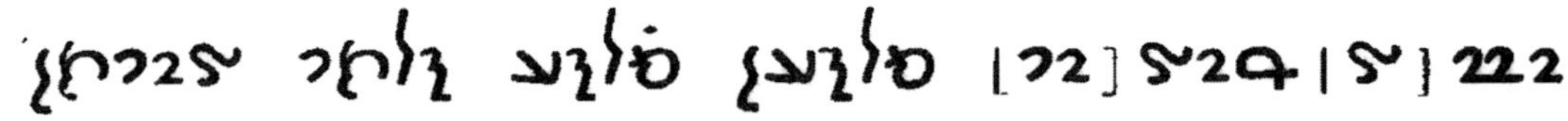
û Sha(h)pûh(rî) malkân malkâ kaltî havîtun; 'and Shâpûr was made king of kings'.

Lin. 3. 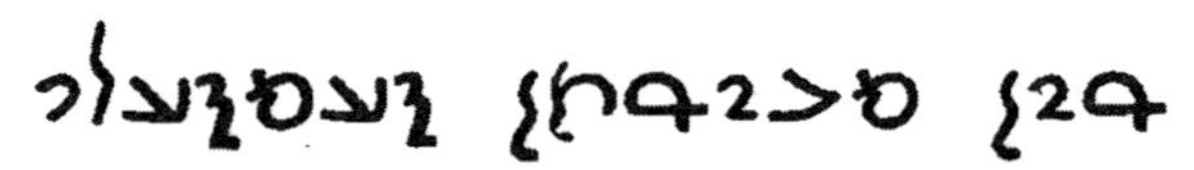 *pavan magûpatan kâmkâlî*; 'on the desire of the mobeds'. The first and last words are quite clear and unmistakeable; the fourth character of the second word is indistinct, but it is most probably a distorted  *p*; the omission of the  in the plural termination is unusual, but it may be a mistake of the transcriber.

Some more words, and even a whole phrase, have been explained by E. W. West, in his paper mentioned above; but as the lines are much mutilated, I refrain from any further remarks.

The Pâi-Kûli inscriptions would afford even more interest than that of Naksh-i Rustam, if they were only available in a more connected form. They consist of thirty-two small fragments, twenty-two of them being in the Sasanian, and ten in the Chaldæo-Pahlavî character. They were discovered and copied for the first time (in 1844) by Sir Henry Rawlinson, who permitted E. Thomas to publish them, in his 'Early Sasanian Inscriptions', with some explanatory remarks. The Sasanian-Pahlavî fragments are printed by him in the Pahlavî type of the books, with two or three additional characters, and the Chaldæo-Pahlavî in Hebrew type; but an accurate fac-simile of the original copies would have been preferred by decipherers. From a note, by the discoverer, appended to the publication, we learn that the stones on which the inscriptions were found, seemed to have belonged to the eastern wall of an ancient fire-temple which crowned the summit of a hill, near the Persian and Turkish frontier and not far from Sulimanieh.

The date of the inscription, to which these fragments belonged, cannot be exactly ascertained. Two names occur with the royal title, viz. *Artakhshatr malkân malkâ* (1, 2.) and *Shahîpûhar malkâ* (25, 6.); whence we must conclude that the inscription cannot be anterior to the time of Shâpûr I.; there is also the name *Aûharmazdî* to be met with (11, 3.), but without the royal title; we cannot, therefore, be certain whether it refers to Hormazd, the successor of Shâpûr, or not. I am rather inclined to assign, to this inscription, a later date than that of Shâpûr I., as we find at least one instance of an Iranian termination added to a Semitic verb, which is never the case in the Sasanian version of the Hâjiâbâd inscription; this is the word [Pahlavi] *yakhshûnt* (7, 5.) probably standing for [Pahlavi] *yakhsûnt* = [Pahlavi] 'he had'; in other cases the terminations are not used, comp. [Pahlavi] *vâkhdûn* (3, 5.) = [Pahlavi] *vâgûnt*, 'he seized, took'; [Pahlavi] *yahvûn* (17, 5. 18, 2.) = [Pahlavi] *yehevûnt*, 'it is'; [Pahlavi] *hûman* (22, 1.) = [Pahlavi], is also used without a suffix. But the inscription is probably older than those of Naksh-i Rustam and Naksh-i Rajab, as they exhibit the addition of the Iranian suffixes to nearly all the Semitic verbs; its date may therefore be in the period between Shâpûr I. and Behram II.

It is very difficult to discover even the general nature of the inscription. It appears to have been a historical record, as different nations and countries are mentioned in it; thus, we have [Pahlavi] (3, 4.) = پارسی

Pârsî, 'a Persian', or (as the final *k* is wanting) 'Persia'; [illegible] [illegible] (1, 3. 6, 5.) *Aîrân shatrî*, אריאן השתר (27, 2. 32, 4.) = [illegible] [illegible] *Aîrân shatru*, ایران شهر 'the Iranian country'; [illegible] [illegible] (5, 3.) *Sakân malkâ*, 'the king of the Sakas', who were probably the inhabitants of Sejestân, the Sakastene of the Greeks; [illegible] [illegible] (7, 3,) *Abîrân malkâ*, 'the king of the Abîrs', who were very likely the Abhîras, at the mouth of the Indus; [illegible] 2 [illegible] [illegible] (15, 3.) *Dûrtân û Pârdân malkâ*, 'king of the Dûrds (probably Kûrds, [illegible] being written for [illegible]) and of the Pârdas'; אתר סורין (32, 2.) *âtar Sûrîn*, 'the country of the Syrians'; פארס (32, 3.) *Pârs*, 'Persia'; אסור (32, 3.) *Asûr*, 'Assyria'; ארמינר (32, 4.) *Armînar*, 'Armenia',

Besides the royal title, several others occur; thus, we find [illegible] (8, 4.) *barbîtâ*, 'chief, general' (for its etymology, see pag. 53); רב השתר (24, 2.) *rab khshatr*, 'the head of the country'; [illegible] (2, 1.) (*âî*)*harpat*, هربد 'a priest of the lowest grade, a herbad; [illegible] (9, 3. 6. 18, 3.) *halgûpat*, or *khargûpat*, the name of a dignity no longer known. Of great interest is the word [illegible] (15. 4.) *zûlâdacht*, in which hardly any other name can be recognised than that of *Zaradusht*, 'Zoroaster' the substitution of [illegible] for [illegible] is not surprising, as in the Chaldæo-Pahlavi, *ch* is frequently replaced by *sh*, comp. *shîhar* for *chitri*. This name is preceded by the words [illegible] [illegible] *bagdat zî*; *bagdat* can hardly be anything else but the Zand *bagô-dâta*, 'created by God'.

Of the other words which may be identified in the inscription, the following are the most interesting: *Aharmanî û shîdân* (3, 2.) 'Ahrîman and the devils' ([illegible], see index, pag. 209); *shapîl* (1, 5.) = [illegible] 'good'; *napshman* (14, 3. 26, 2.) = [illegible]; and *benapshman* (15, 5.) = [illegible] 'himself, own'. In the Chaldæo-Pahlavî portion, we meet with *yehût* (25, 5.) = *yahvûn* (see pag. 59), *haqâîmû* (26, 3.; see pag. 55), and *havîndî* (27, 5.; see pag. 59—60).

All the other Sasanian inscriptions, which are known, are either too much mutilated, or too short (containing nothing but names and titles)

to be now of any value for judging of the character of the Pahlavî language; I therefore confine myself to enumerating them. There are two short inscriptions of *Ardeshîr Bâbegân* (A. D. 226 — 238) at Naksh-i Rustam, in three languages (Flandin, vol. IV. pl. 181ter); the Greek and Sasanian texts of one of them have been given in full, on pag. 4; each of them has, besides the Sasanian text, a Chaldæo-Pahlavî and a Greek version. There is also a short inscription of Shâpûr I. (A. D. 238—269) in three languages, at Naksh-i Rajab (Flandin, vol. IV. pl. 190); besides two inscriptions at Tâk-i Bustân, near Kirmanshah, which are in Sasanian Pahlavî only, one of Shâpûr II. (A. D. 310—381) and the other of Shâpûr III. (A. D. 385 — 390), and which were deciphered by Sylvestre de Sacy (see pag. 5); an inscription of Narses, [illegible] *Narsahî*, (A. D. 291—300) at Shâhpûr (Flandin, pl. 45); and two inscriptions of Shâpûr II. and Shâpûr III. at Persepolis, of which the copies made by Sir W. Ouseley (Travels, vol. II. pl. 42) are only partially legible [1]).

Besides the Sasanian inscriptions found in Persia (of which more might be discovered if they were systematically sought for), there are some Pahlavî inscriptions in India, of a later date, which deserve a passing notice.

In the caves of Kanheri, near Bombay, five inscriptions in the Pahlavî character have been found, and fac-similes of them were published in the Zartosht-i Abhyâsa (1866, pag. 98 and 146), a Guzerâti journal, edited by Khursedji Rustemji Câma, and devoted to the discussion of subjects bearing on the Zoroastrian religion and Iranian languages; attempts were also made at deciphering these inscriptions; in the same journal (pag. 100—103, 146—164 and 209—217). Two of them had been transcribed by E. W. West, who furnished the Bombay Branch of the Royal Asiatic Society with copies of them, and pointed out the existence of a third which is illegible; the other two were discovered by Bhâû Dâjî. They are all dated, but it is difficult to decipher some of the

---

1) All these Inscriptions will be found in E. Thomas's 'Early Sasanian Inscriptions'.

numerals; the first figures, in each date, are clearly the number [illegible] *300*, but the tens and units which follow the hundreds, are not very legible, and can be differently interpreted. The date in No. 1. is probably 364 Yazdagird (A. D. 995); in No. 3. are the words [illegible] [illegible] [illegible] [illegible] [illegible] *shanat 390 Yazdagird shatrûyâr* (شهریار) 'the year 390 (A. D. 1021) of Yazdagird the king', the name of this last Iranian king being abbreviated [1]). Three of the inscriptions record the names of Parsis who visited the caves in the latter part of the 10th and beginning of the 11th century. The characters resemble very closely, in shape, those used in the oldest extant MSS. which belong to the 14th century. And the language is identical with that of the books; comp. No. 1. lin. 3—4: [illegible] [illegible] [illegible] [illegible] [illegible] 'they came to this place'; in lin. 13. there is the name [illegible] 'Hormazd', written in the same way as in the books.

Of more interest is a Pahlavî inscription found on a copper plate in the south of India. It forms part of a grant which records the rights and privileges of the early Christians on the Malabar coast. The grant is engraved on six copper plates, five of which contain, in old Tamil characters, the grant made by an ancient king, to the Christian congregation of his country; the sixth contains the names of the witnesses, in three different characters and languages, none of them Indian, viz. eleven names in the Kufic character and Arabic language, ten in the Sasanian Pahlavî character and language, and four in the Hebrew (Chaldæo-Pahlavî?) character and the Persian language. Facsimiles of the whole inscription on the six plates, were published in the 7th volume of the Journal of the Royal Asiatic Society of Great Britain (pag. 343); its date cannot be ascertained until the inscription shall have been deciphered, but we shall not be far wrong if we assume it to belong to the 9th century [2]).

---

1) In the MSS. it is generally written [illegible] (as in the colophon to a fine copy of the Yasna with Pahlavî translation in my possession) and this is frequently read *shakant*, but this is wrong, as it is followed by *malkân malkâ;* it should be read *yajdakart* which is a corruption of *yazdakirt*.

2) See the Memoir of the Primitive Church of Malayâla, or of the Syrian

Each attestation in the Sasanian Pahlavî is introduced by the words *mînûkû lî*, then follows the name in full, succeeded each time by the phrase *patash gôkâs hûmanam*, 'I am witness to it'; which language is identical with that of the books. As regards *mînûkû*, it can only be taken as a title which is attributed to every witness, and which contains the *minû*, 'spirit', of the early Sasanian inscriptions; which follows, is לי 'I'; and the whole means 'the spirit of me, my spirit', i. e. I myself; *mînû* always signifying the invisible counterpart of anything visible on this earth (see above, pag. 50); for *gôkâs*, 'witness', see the index, pag. 121. The names are difficult to read, and do not look like common Parsi names, nor are they Christian; in lin. 13, 'Ormazd' is clearly legible, which indicates a true Parsi name. E. W. West has made an attempt at reading almost all the names, but as they are neither legibly written, nor familiar to us, I do not think it safe to venture on an explanation of them. The shape of the letters is nearly the same as in the books, and the compound characters are employed throughout.

Regarding the signatures in the Hebrew character, which have been all read by E. W. West, in his paper on the Sasanian inscriptions, the names חסן עלי *Hasan 'Alî*, מיכאיל *Mîkâîl* (Michael) and אברהם *Abraham* are pretty clear. Each signature is introduced by the phrase הכ גון כן *hak-gûn kun*, which is translated by E. W. West as 'the truth-speaking-doer'. To this interpretation, which appears somewhat artificial, I cannot give my full assent; I quite agree with taking *kun* as identical with the Persian کن 'making, doing', *in fine compositorum;* but *gûn* cannot be taken in the sense of 'speaking', as this would be *gû* alone, but not *gûn;* besides, I doubt if the Arabic word حقّ 'truth' were used at so early a time in Persian. I am however, unable to offer any satisfactory explanation; I take *hak* as identical with the Chaldee הָךְ 'this', and *gûn* as the Persian گون 'manner, mode, way'; the whole would thus mean: 'doing

---

Christians of the Apostle Thomas, by Charles Swanston, in the Journal of the Roy. As. Soc. vol. I. pag. 177.

in this manner', i. e. hereby (by the signature which follows). Each signature is followed by the words בדיש גוהם *badîsh guvaham*, 'I am witness to it'; *badîsh* is equivalent to *patash* in the Sasanian signatures, and *guvaham* to *gôkas hûmanam; guvah* being Pers. گُواه 'testimony, a witness', and the suffix *am* is 'I am'. These readings show that the writers did not use the Hebrew language; for the language here is clearly Persian, but in a form which closely approaches to the so-called Chaldæo-Pahlavî which appears, from this document, to have been still in use in the 9th century, among certain classes of the inhabitants of Persia. For all those who signed the grant as witnesses, seem to have come from Persia and Arabia, and were probably emigrants.

4. On the character of the Pahlavî languages.

From the preceding section any reader, who is somewhat acquainted with Pahlavî, will readily perceive that the language of the Sasanian inscriptions does not materially differ from that of the books, and that since the close of the 3d century, the former may even be considered as identical with the latter. There is not much difference observable between the Sasanian version of the Hâjîâbâd inscription, and the language of the later inscriptions and books; but this difference is of great importance, as it enables us to judge of the true character of the Pahlavî language. I shall therefore proceed to point out all those differences which bear materially on the subject, by summing up the results of the preceding investigation and enlarging on them.

a) The principal difference consists in the fact, that the Iranian verbal terminations, such as *t, d* (in the 3d person), are wanting (in connection with the Semitic verbs) throughout the Sasanian version of the Hâjîâbâd inscription, though there would have been occasion to employ them; whilst they are used throughout the Pahlavî of the books. This inscription belongs to the reign of Shâpûr I., and consequently to about the middle of the 3d century A. D. In the Pâi Kûlî inscription, which follows next in age (belonging probably to the reign of Hormazd I. the successor of Shâpûr I.), the Iranian terminations are also wanting in most cases, being only occasionally added. In the Naksh-i Rustam and Naksh-i Rajab inscriptions, which date from the end of the 3[d] century, we find the verbal terminations *m*, *t*, *d* frequently added, though in about as many instances omitted. This omission is constant in the case of *yahvûn*, to which no termination has been found joined; the forms *yahvûnt*, *yahvûnad* being thus entirely excluded from the inscriptions; while on the other hand *yahvûn* is never found in the books, except perhaps in the sense of an imperative; in none of the sentences, in which *yahvûn* occurs in the inscriptions, can it be taken as an imperative, but only as a third person, or past participle. Similarly, the characteristic of the 3[d] person, *d*, or *t* (which appear to be used indifferently) is always wanting, in the inscriptions, in the case of *hûman*; whereas in the books, *d* is always added, forming ; but in the first person, *m* is added, just as *m* is in the books.

b) In the Hâjîâbâd inscription, no Iranian suffix is added to a particle, as is the case in the later inscriptions and throughout the books. There are two instances in which a suffix is used after a particle, in H., viz. *âpan* and *âdînan* (see pag. 51. 53); but *an* is clearly the Semitic suffix of the 1st pers. plur., and corresponds to *mân* = مان in the Pahlavî of the books, so that = , and = . In the Naksh-i Rustam, Pâî Kûlî and Naksh-i Rajab inscriptions, there are *âpam* = , and *âpash* = , by which the personal pronouns of the 1st and 3[d] persons singular are expressed.

c) The final *u* of the Pahlavî books, is wanting throughout the Sasanian inscriptions of the 3[d] century, but it is found on the coins of the 6th century, e. g. in = افزود. In the early inscriptions, *î* is found in place of *u*, as in N. Raj. we have *kaltî hûmanam* = *kartu hûmanam*, see pag. 72.

d) No clear trace of the *idhâfat* is to be found in the Sasanian inscriptions, whereas it is always employed in the books. The final *î*, which frequently occurs, *never* represents the Persian *idhâfat.* According to the rules prevailing in Pâzand and Persian, the *idhâfat* would be unmistakeably necessary before *Aîrân,* in the phrase: *malkân malkâ Aîrân û Anîrân,* 'the king of kings of Iran and Aniran'; also in *barman mazdayasn,* 'the son of the Hormazd-worshipper', and in *napî bagî Pâpakî,* 'the grandson of the divine being Pâpak', (all from the Hâjîâbâd inscription) the *idhâfat* would be necessary, but does not exist, for the *î* in *napî,* in the last phrase, is a common termination where no *idhâfat* is requisite, as in the words *bagî Pâpakî* and *Shahpûhrî,* in the same inscription.

e) The termination *shn, eshn,* which is so frequent in the Pahlavî of the books, has not yet been discovered in the inscriptions.

Whilst the differences between the Sasanian Pahlavî and that of the books, are comparatively trifling, it is not so with the Chaldæo-Pahlavî. It is true that this language also stands near to that of the books, but it cannot be shown to be in any way identical with the latter, as has been the case with Sasanian Pahlavî since the end of the 3d century. It had, no doubt, a similar origin; but there are nevertheless differences observable not only in the use of words, but also in the forms; the most noteworthy of these deviations, both from the Sasanian Pahlavî and from that of the books, I shall now proceed to point out.

a) Nouns. The nouns in *man* = , which are so frequent in the Sasanian Pahlavî and in the books, are much more rare in the Chaldæo-Pahlavî; thus we have *yadâ* instead of *yadman* = , *nagarîn* instead of *ragalman* = , and *barî* instead of *barman* = ; but the termination *man* is preserved in *zanman* = = 'this', and also occurs in *qadmatman* and *panman* which have not been found in Sasanian Pahlavî and the books. The plural is formed both in *în* and *ân,* whilst in S. P. and the MSS. only the form in *ân* is used; e. g. *malkîn,* S. P. *malkân*; *khshatardarîn,* S. P. *shataldalân*; and *nagarîn,* 'feet'; also *rabân* and *barbîtân.* The *idhâfat* seems to be wanting in the same cases as in S. P.; but the *î* in *barî* might be explained as such, if we did not find the phrase ***barî le-barî*** for 'grandson', in the Chaldæo-version of the short tri-lingual inscription of Naksh-i Rajab (see Flandin, Voy. en Perse, vol. 4. pl. 190), where the first *î* would be superfluous as an *idhâfat.* Somewhat remarkable is the insertion of *î* after the first part of a compound noun, e. g. *pûhrî-pûhar*, 'the son of the son', i. e. grandson, and *Shahîpûhar*, Shahpûhr = Shâpûr; here it is comparable with the *î* in the first part of compound Hebrew and Phenician names, e. g. מַלְכִּיצֶדֶק, אֱלִיעֶזֶר, עַמִּינָדָב, חַנִּיבַעַל 'Hannibal'. The final *î* of S. P., and the corresponding [illegible] *u* of the later coins and in the MSS. seem to be almost entirely wanting; thus we have *bag* instead of *bagî*, *Shahîpûhar* instead of *Shahpûhrî*, ***Pâpak*** instead of ***Pâpakî***, and ***shîhar*** instead of *chitrî;* in *karzâvanî* and ***shîtî*** the final *î* forms probably part of the termination itself; *barî* and *ârqî* appear to be exceptions.

b) Pronouns. These differ but little; in Ch. P. we have *lan*, 'to us, by us, we', instead of [illegible] = [illegible] *lanman* (*roman*). As a demonstrative we find *hû, hûb, hûp* (Heb. הוא), instead of [illegible] in S. P., which latter is, however, also used in Ch. P.; *hû* is probably identical with [illegible] of the books, which is generally read *gho*, or *ghan; ânû* is also used in the same sense. The *pronomina suffixa* joined to particles, seem to be entirely wanting in Ch. P.; we cannot therefore decide whether Semitic, or Iranian, pronominal suffixes were used; *âpan* in S. is simply expressed by *lan*, and the suffix in *âdînan* is omitted along with the particle; no traces of forms like *âpam* and *âpash*, have been yet discovered. The few pronouns which have been found, are all Semitic, just as in S.

c) Verbs. In these more differences are observable than in the other parts of speech. The termination *ûn, un,* which is added to all the Semitic verbs in S. P. and the MSS., is wanting throughout; thus, we find *yehût* instead of [illegible] *yahvûn*, *haqâîmût* instead of [illegible] *hanakhtûn*, *ramît* instead of [illegible] *ramîtun*, and *shadît* instead of [illegible] *shadîtun;* we have also *havînt* and *havîndî* instead of [illegible] *hûman*. All the Semitic verbs in Ch., except *kadab* (*katab*) and *shadîû*

(3[d] pers. plur.), have the termination *t, d,* or *dí,* which is entirely wanting in the Sasanian version of the Hâjiâbâd inscription, and only optionally used in the later inscriptions. There are some slight differences to be observed in the tenses in which the verbs are taken from the Semitic languages; in S. P. and the MSS. دوانیمن *yekavîmûn,* the imperfect of Pael of the root קום 'to stand', is used for the Iranian *stâ,* استادن; while in Ch. P. we find only the perfect of the Hifil, *haqâîmû.*

d) Prepositions and particles. Instead of S. ‫לז‬ *ûl,* we find Ch. *kal* = על; both are probably identical, but the Ch. represents by *k* a harsher pronunciation of the original ע. The preposition *le* (without suffixes) = Heb. Chald לְ, seems to have been of pretty frequent use in Ch., as a sign of the accusative (Hâj. lin. 7. 14.), whilst it is not used in S. in the same cases; it is also once used in connection with a verbal form (Hâj. Ch. lin. 8.), and once with an infinitive (lin. 7.), at it is also in S. lin. 7. There is *patan*, or perhaps *pavîn*, as the characters may also be read, for S. *pavan*; *qadmatman* for S. *lûînî*, 'before'; *âk* for S. *hat; hîp* for S. *âyû;* while *bîsh* is something peculiar, as it may be the preposition *be* = בְּ with a suffix (see pag. 57).

e) In the use of words there also exist, of course, some differences, but they are by no means great. In S., as well as in Ch., both Semitic and Iranian words are freely used. We find Iranian words in S. represented by other Iranian words in Ch.; as *pûhrî-pûhar*, 'grandson', for S. *napî*; *vîm*, 'cave', for S. *dîkî*; and *aûpdasht*, 'ordered', for S. *parmât.* Sometimes an Iranian word in S. is represented by a Semitic word in Ch.; thus we find *âlahâ,* 'divine being', for S. *bagî;* and *banît*, 'constructed', for S. *chîtî.* And sometimes a Semitic word in S. is represented by another Semitic word in Ch.; thus *hararyâ*, 'an arrow', occurs for S. *hatyâ;* and *qadmatman*, 'before', for S. *lûînî.* But the bulk of the words seem to be identical in Ch. and S.

From these observations we are justified in drawing the inference, that the Sasanian-Pahlavî and Chaldæo-Pahlavî are two very closely allied dialects, which can have had, on the whole, but *one* origin. Both contain

Iranian as well as Semitic elements, but the latter far outweigh the former; thus we find, in the S. version of the Hâjîâbâd inscription, about three-fourths, and in the Ch. version four-fifths, of the words are of Semitic origin. This result makes the Iranian character of Pahlavi, at the very outset, exceedingly doubtful; but notwithstanding the great preponderance of Semitic words, this character might nevertheless be granted to it, if it could be shown that its grammar, and specially those parts of speech which determine the character of languages (such as pronouns, or case signs) were of Iranian origin.

As the whole question about the character of the language, depends upon its grammar, I shall proceed to discuss briefly all the points which bear upon it; using, of course, indiscriminately the two inscriptional languages, as well as that of the MSS., but laying stress principally on the first two, as the last has been gradually undergoing a change from a Semetico-Iranian into a purely Iranian language.

a) Declension of nouns.

There is no distinction of genders, as there is in Zand, old-Persian and the Semitic languages; in this respect the Pahlavi of the 3d century was already reduced to the same state in which we find the Armenian in the oldest documents. The dual number of the older Iranian and the Semitic languages has also entirely disappeard.

To express the plural, the termination *ân* is alone used in the Sasanian Pahlavi; but in the Chaldæo-Pahlavi *în* is used as well as *ân*. In the MSS. we find *ân* nearly everywhere, though the termination *îhâ* has occasionally crept in, as in Bundeh. 19, 1. we find *kûpîhâ*, 'mountains', but in 18, 14. we have *ân* first added, forming *kûpânîhâ*; also in the Pahl.-Pâz. Gl. 3, 3. we have *mîvêhâ*, 'fruits', and 4, 7. *tarîhâ*, 'vegetables'. This termination *îhâ* is no doubt identical with the modern Persian *hâ*, and its frequent occurence in the headings to the chapters of the Pahl.-Pâz. Gl., is owing to their being really modern Persian written in Pahlavi characters, and therefore proving nothing as to the termination in Sasanian Pahlavî. In the MSS. we find the termination *ân*, which is chiefly confined to animate objects in modern Persian, used also for all other nouns, as in ﺳﻨﺘﻤﺴﻮ *shanatânu*, 'years'.

This plural termination *ân* is generally explained as a remnant of the old-Persian and Zand genetive plural termination *anăm*; but this derivation, though at first sight it seems probable, is open to objections. Firstly, the proper termination of the genetive plural, in the old Iranian languages, is not *anăm*, but *ăm; anăm* being only used with nouns whose crude forms end in *a*, or *â*. Secondly, a final *m* in the ancient languages, is generally not changed to *n* in modern Persian; against this assertion, the defenders of the current explanation would, no doubt, adduce the enclitic particle *shâm* = *eshâm* in old-Persian, and identify it with the modern Persian شان *shân* which has the same meaning; but this identification is merely illusory, as the *ân* in *shân*, is only the ordinary plural sign added to the singular شَ 'he, she, it'. As no sound reasons can be given for an Iranian derivation of the plural termination *ân*, I do not hesitate to trace it to a Semitic source. In the Assyrian, the emphatic plural actually ends in *ân*, or with the case signs, in *ânu* = ﺳﻮ, *âni* and *âna*, (see Ménant, Grammaire assyrienne, pag. 60—61); in Chaldee the pl. of the fem. is also *ân*; we also find it in Ethiopic, where it is used for the formation of the plural of adjectives and participles (see Dillmann, Grammatik der äthiopischen Sprache, pag. 230). The termination *în* of the Chaldæo-Pahlavî is used in Chaldee and Syriac as the characteristic of the plural.

The cases of the nouns are not expressed by any terminations; those which existed in old-Persian and Zand, have entirely disappeared in Pahlavi, and even in the inscriptions of the 3d century, there is not the slightest trace of them. This would be very remarkable if we considered Pahlavî as an Iranian language, for even the Armenian has preserved several case terminations, and in English some traces of them exist. There are two vowels found at the end of nouns, viz. *î* in the Sasanian Pahlavî, and *û* in the later Sasanian and MSS., which might be taken for case endings; but it would be hardly possible to trace them to any Iranian language, whereas they can be explained from the Semitic languages, just as simply as the plural in *ân*. The final *î* is nothing but the Semitic vowel *i*, *î*, expressing the genitive case, or connection of one noun with another. It occurs in Hebrew, Phenician, Arabic and Assyrian, but only in Arabic is the use of this *i* (*in* if no article precedes) strictly defined; it is there only used when the noun is preceded by another, on which it depends, or by a preposition; it is thus the proper genitive case, and also the case governed by prepositions. In Hebrew *î* is occasionally used as a connecting vowel in old passages, as well as in poetical ones. It connects: *a*) one noun with another, without any intervening preposition, e. g. Deut. 33, 16 וּרְצוֹן שֹׁכְנִי סְנֶה 'and the pleasure of him who dwells in the thorny bush', Gen. 31, 39 גְּנֻבְתִי יוֹם וּגְנֻבְתִי לָיְלָה 'what was stolen by day and what was stolen at night', Is. 1, 21 מְלֵאֲתִי מִשְׁפָּט 'full of justice'; *b*) also with an intervening preposition e. g. Is. 22, 16 חֹקְקִי בַסֶּלַע 'excavating in the rock', Gen. 49, 11 אֹסְרִי לַגֶּפֶן 'tying to the vine'; *c*) the components of compound proper names, see pag. 85; *d*) and is added to some prepositions, such as בִּלְתִּי 'without', זוּלָתִי 'except'. In Phenician the connective *î* is not unfrequent in proper names, as in Hann-i-bal, Idd-i-bal and In-i-bal; whether it was also used in appellatives, cannot be ascertained, as in Phenician writing final vowels are not expressed by a separate character, (see more on the subject in Schröder, Die Phönizische Sprache, pag. 177—179). In Assyrian, *i* is frequently added at the end of a noun, and was originally intended for expressing the genitive case, just as in Arabic; but this rule was not strictly observed, even in the inscriptions of Nineveh, as the *i* could occasionally interchange with *u*, which was originally the sign of the nominative, or with *a* which was intended for the accusative; thus we find frequently *sar Babilu*, 'king of Babylon', instead of *sar Babili* [1]). As regards the final و *u*, I have

---

1) Regarding the Assyrian case terminations, see Ménant, Grammaire assyrienne, pag. 58—67; Oppert, Élémens de la grammaire assyrienne, 2d ed. pag. 104—105; and J. Olshausen, Abhandlungen der Königl. Akademie der Wissenschaften zu Berlin, for 1864, pag. 485—486.

treated of it already in the introduction to the Zand-Pahlavi glossary, pag. XXIV—XXVI. It was originally the sign of the nominative, as in Arabic and Assyrian (in Hebrew a connecting nowel like ʾ); it occurs in the *earliest* Pahlavi writing, on the Abd-Zohar coins of the 4th century B. C. In the course of time this *u* seems to have become, in Pahlavi, an indistinct vowel at the end of nouns, infinitives and participles, which was either dropped in modern Persian, or represented by a short *a*, or *e*, e. g. [illegible], کرده *karda*, or *karde*, 'made'. It appears that the difference between *i* and *u* was not clearly appreciated in Sasanian times, for in the inscriptions we find *î* employed generally in cases in which only [illegible] *u* is used in the later inscriptions and MSS.

A trace of this final vowel *i*, or *u*, seems still left in modern Persian, in the *idhâfat*, which I unhesitatingly trace to it, and which is generally not expressed in writing, but is sounded like *e* by the Parsi priests in India, who consider that the only correct pronunciation. I am fully aware that linguists are now accustomed to take this *e*, *i*, as a corruption of the Zand relative *ya*, which is often syntactically used in the same manner as the Persians employ the *idhâfat*. But this derivation is open to grave objections; firstly, the *idhâfat* must, if it be the remnant of a relative pronoun, be traced to the old-Persian, and not to the Zand; now in old-Persian, the relative is *hya* in the nominative singular, and *tya* in the other cases; if therefore the *idhâfat* were derived from it, we should expect to find it in the form *he*, *hî*, or *te*, *tî*, but not in that of a short *e*, or *i*. Secondly, if the derivation from the Zand *ya* were correct, we should have it in the form *je*; for an initial *y* is not lost in Persian, but generally becomes *j*; we also find that the initial sound of the interrogative *ka* has been preserved in the modern Persian که *ke*, which has taken the place of the ancient relative which has been lost altogether. Thirdly, if the *idhâfat* be derived from the ancient Iranian relative, it seems impossible to account for its almost total absence in the inscriptions of the third century A. D., as in that case we might look, with some degree of certainty, for a form like *hî*, or *tî*; for if the old-Persian *Artakhshatra* has undergone only the slight change to *Artakhshatr*, we might fully expect that the relative would not be further altered than to *hî*, or *tî*, in the inscriptions; but no trace of such a relative can be discovered in them; the relative employed in the inscriptions, is *zî* which is of Semitic origin, and in the books, *zî* and *mûn* (also Semitic). Having shown the improbability of the derivation of the *idhâfat* from the Zand relative *ya*, for reasons which I think conclusive, I shall briefly state my own opinion as to its origin. I consider that it originated in the old Semitic termination *i* of the genitive case, which was, in the course of time, used freely for all cases, and especially when a noun was followed by another noun in the genitive case, or by an adjective; in the third century A. D. the use of *i*, specially as a sign of the genitive, appears to have been very rare; but the Persians accustomed themselves to use it generally as a connecting vowel; and as Pahlavî passed gradually into modern Persian, this vowel was retained and its grammatical function fixed. In the Pahlavî of the books, *e*, *i* is generally used before the genitive, though some prepositions, such as *min*, *yin* and *avu* = Pâz. *ôi*, are sometimes employed, in the translations, to express the genitive case in Zand; if the genitive precedes the noun, on which it depends, its relation is not expressed by any particle, e. g. *malkân malkâ*, 'king of kings'.

The accusative case is not distinguished in the Pahlavî of books, except occasionally by the postposition *râi* (see the index, pag. 195—196); in Chald.-Pahl. *le* = Heb. לְ is sometimes used to denote this case. The dative is distinguished by the particle *val*, *ûl*, Heb. Chald. על (see index, pag. 226); as this is read *ôi* by the Parsis, we often find *avu* = Z. *avi*, Pâz. *ôi*, substituted for it, but no instance of such substitution has been found in the inscriptions. Instead of we find occasionally *valman*, *ûlman* (*varman*, see index, pag. 227), but this is a demonstrative pronoun, and when used as a sign of the dative, it must be a misreading for ; it must be the same with the demonstrative *ghû* (*ghan*, see index, pag. 123) which we also find occasionally used as a sign of the dative. In the Sas.-Pahl. we find = , and in Chald.-Pahl. *kal*, which are only various orthographies for על. The ablative case is distinguished by the preposition = Heb. מִן, and the locative by *yin* (which the Parsis read *dayen,* see index, pag. 106—107).

The adjective, when it follows its substantive, is connected therewith by means of the *idhâfat*; but in the Sasanian inscriptions no certain traces of this can be discovered. This practice of joining an adjective to its substantive, by means of a connective vowel, has its analogy in the Assyrian, e. g. *sarru rabu,* 'the great king', not *sar rabu.* Comparative and superlative suffixes have not yet been discovered in the inscriptions; in the MSS. they are *tar* = Z. Sans. *tara* and *tum* = Z. *tema,* Sans. *tama.* There are however instances, in which the comparison is expressed, not by any suffix added to the adjective, but simply by the preposition *min*, just as in the Semitic languages, for instance Vend. 2, 37. (Sp.): *adinu Jam denman damîk barâ sâtûnînît khaduk sarûishûtak min zak mas chîgûn pêsh min zak yehvûntu,* 'then Jamshîd made this earth burst asunder by one third larger than this (was), that it was (larger) than this (was) before'. This way of expressing the comparison is evidently not Iranian, but clearly betrays a Semitic origin.

b) Pronouns.

In both versions of the Hâjîâbâd inscription, the pronouns, without exception, are Semitic, and agree with those in the MSS.; even the *pronomina suffixa,* in this inscription, are thoroughly Semitic (see pag. 51—52, with regard to *âpan*), whilst in the Sasanian inscriptions of the latter end of the third century, they are already Iranian, just as in the books.

Personal pronouns. 1st pers. sing. S. and Ch. *lî*, P. 'I' (to be read *li,* comp. لِی *lîj*, and see the index, pag. 189—190 and 196) = Heb. Chald. לִי 'to me'. 1st pers. pl. S. *lanman*, Ch. *lan*, P. *lanman*, 'we' (see *rôman* in the index, pag. 198) = Chald. לָן 'to us'.

2^d^ pers. sing. P. *lak* = Chald. לָךְ 'to thee'. 2^d^ pers. pl. P. *lakôm* = Chald. לְכוֹם, Heb. לָכֶם 'to you'. 3^d^ pers. sing. S. *ûlman*, Ch. *hû*, *hûp*, *hûb*, P. *ûlman* (see *varman* in the index, pag. 227) = Assyr. אִל, 'he, she, it'; P. *ânu*, probably identical with the demonstrative *ânu* = Syr. הָנּוֹן; P. *ghû* (see *ghan* in the index, pag. 123) = Ch. *hû*, *hûp*, Heb. Chald. הוּא. 3^d^ pers. pl. P. *ûlmanshân* 'they, those' (with the Iranian pl. suff. *shân*). Regarding the origin of the pronouns of the 1st and 2^d^ persons, they are all Semitic dative cases, formed by the addition of the pronominal suffixes to the preposition לְ; their application as nominatives may be easily accounted for, by the fact that they are chiefly used in connection with past participles; this is evident from the inscriptional Pahlavî, comp. the Ch. version of the Hâj. inscr. lin. 5: *âmat lan zanman hararyâ shadît*, 'when this arrow was shot by us', i. e. when we shot this arrow, which would be expressed in the Pahlavî of the MSS. by *âmat lanman denmen tîr shadîtûnt* 1); comp. also the S. version, lin. 11: *âkhar lanman parmât (farmât)* 'afterwards it was ordered by us', i. e. we ordered. The termination = *man*, in = and = , is remarkable; it frequently occurs in nouns, but only in words of Semitic origin, and its derivation will be discussed hereafter.

Besides the personal pronouns above mentioned, there is in Pahlavî a set of pronouns which are joined to particles, especially to *ap*, and as they stand at the beginning of sentences they may be taken as equivalent to the others. The suffixed pronouns in the Sasanian version of the Hâj. insc., are only Semitic; they are *âpan*, 'we', and *âdînan*, 'then

1) A striking analogy is offered by the modern Indian vernaculars, which prefer a passive construction with the subject in the instrumental, instead of the nominative case, in all tenses formed from the past participles of transitive verbs; thus the phrase, 'what fault has he committed'? is expressed in Hindûstânî by *us-ne kyâ taksîr kî hai?* in Marâthî by *tyâ-ne kây aparâdh kelâ âhe?* in Gujarâtî by *eṇe suñ gunâh kidho-chê?* all of which are literally, 'by him what fault is committed'?

we' (see pag. 53). In the later Sasanian inscriptions as well as in the MSS. they are only Iranian; the complete set, with *ap*, is as follows: 1st pers. sing. *apam* = S., pl. *apmân*; 2d pers. sing. *apat*, pl. *aptân*; 3d pers. sing. *apash* = S., pl. *apshân*. The particle *ap*, to which 1st *am*, *mân*, 2d *at*, *tân*, 3d *ash*, *shân* are joined, is however Semitic (see pag. 51). They are not confined to this particle, but are also joined to *amat*, 'when', *aígh*, 'that, thus', *meman*, 'what', *adín*, 'then', *mûn*, 'who', and کی *zí*, 'which' (see *zíam* in the index, pag. 242); also even to prepositions, as *pavan*, 'in', which are all likewise of Semitic origin. Sometimes they are joined to nouns and verbs, as is generally the case in modern Persian, where they are not added to the simple prepositions.

The personal pronouns, *li, lak, ûlman, lanman, lakôm, ûlmanshân*, are also used as *possessiva*, without any change, and can be placed either before, or after, the noun. This circumstance is a further proof that they do not represent nominatives, but oblique cases; for if they were nominatives, their proper place would be only after the substantive, with the *idhâfat* intervening, as in modern Persian. There appear however traces of separate possessive pronouns. One instance is *liûman* = *li-hûman* 'belonging to me' i. e. mine (see *ragôman* ind. pag. 191—192); its plural is *liûmanshân* 'ours'.

Demonstratives. S. and Ch. *zak*, P. کو *zak*, دو *dak*, Chald. דֵּךְ; S. and Ch. *zanman*, P. *denman*, Chald. דְּנָא, דֵּן, דֵּין; S. *ûlman*, P. *ûlman*, Assyr. *ul*, Syr. ܗܳܢܘܢ; Ch. *ânû*, P. *ânû*, Syr. ܐܢܘܢ.

Relatives. P. *mûn*, Syr. ܡܰܢ; S. *zí*, P. کی *zí* (used with suffixes), Heb. זֶה, זוּ 1), Chald. דִּי; S., P. *meman* 'which, of what kind', Assyr. *mamman* (see ind. pag. 153—154).

1) זֶה is properly the demonstrative pronoun in Hebrew, but it is sometimes used in the sense of a relative, e. g. Job. 19, 19. Ps. 104, 8. and generally in the form זוּ Ex. 15, 13. Ps. 9, 16. 10, 2. 32, 8. 62, 12.

Interrogatives. P. مون *mûn;* but كتسد *katâr* and كتسم *katâm* are frequently used in this sense, Sans. *katara* and *katama.*

Reciprocals. S. ܢܦܫܡܢ *nafshman,* P. نفشمن, Heb. Chald. נֶפֶשׁ; P. خوت *khût*, Pers. خود; P. خويش *khêsh*, Pers. خويش.

Indefinites. P. كند *kanâ*, Chald. כֹּלָּא 'all, every one'; P. مندوم *mandûm*, Chald. מִדַּעַם 'something', for מִנְדַּעַם; ايش *aîsh*, 'some one', Heb. אִישׁ; زكاى *zakâi*, زك زكاى *zak-î zakâi*, 'another', pl. زكانو *zakânu*, comp. Heb. זֶה — זֶה 'the one — the other' (Ex. 14, 20. Is. 6, 3); زك اند *zak and*, 'as much', in which expression the second part is Iranian (a corruption of *avant*). The other indefinite pronouns are all Iranian: كتارجاى *katarjâi*, 'any one', Z. *katâra* + suff. *jâi*, *châi*, which generalizes; هر *har*, Z. *haurva*; هرويسپ *harvisp*, Z. *haurva* + *vîspa*, هرويسپينو *harvispînu*; هرويست *harvist*, هرويستينو *harvistînu*, in which two latter forms *vist is* only a corruption of *visp*; چيكامجاى *chîkâmjâi*, 'whatever', = *chi* + *kâm* + *jâi*, lit. 'whatever wish'; چانچ *chânach*, 'whichever', Z. *chana*, 'any one', + *cha* which generalizes.

c) Numerals.

Cardinal numbers. The numerals from one to ten are all Semitic, but from eleven upwards they are all Iranian, if written in words and not with numerical symbols. I enumerate those of Semitic origin, both in the form in which they are found in the MSS. and in that used on the Sasanian coins.

1. ادوك *khaduk*, 'one', on the Sasanian coins לעדכו [1]) *âadî* = *âhadî*, Heb. אֶחָד, Chald. חַד, Ethiop. *akhadu* (see index, pag. 49);

---

1) See B. Dorn, Mélanges asiatiques, Tome III. pag. 441—442. He enumerates and examines the different orthographies of the word on coins. ד *d* being often confonnded with ך *k*, as we have already observed in the Sasanian inscriptions, it has been read *aêvak*, but this is untenable; the traditional pronunciation *aduk* contains an indication of its derivation.

2. *talîn*, 'two' S. *talîn*, Chald. תְּרֵין ,תְּרֵי; 3. *taltâ*, 'three', S. *taltâ*, *telat*, Chald. תְּלָת; 4. *arbâ*, 'four', S. *albâ*, *arbâ*, Chald. אַרְבָּע; 5. *khômasyâ*, 'five', S. *khômasâ*, Chald. חַמְשָׁא; 6. *shatâ*, 'six', S. *satâ*; Chald. שִׁתָּא; 7. *shabâ*, 'seven', S. *shabâ*, Chald. שִׁבְעָא; 8. *tômanyâ*, 'eight', S. *tômanâ*, *temanâ*, Chald. תְּמַנְיָא; 9. *tasâ*, 'nine', S. *teshâ*, Chald. תְּשְׁעָה; 10. *asharyâ*, 'ten', S. *asharâ*, Chald. עַסְרָא. The tens, hundreds and thousands are Iranian, and identical with those in modern Persian, see the glossary, pag. 20, and Mordtmann, 'Erklärung der Münzen mit Pehlevi-Legenden' (Zeitschrift der D. Morg. Ges. vol. VIII. Tafel III.)

The ordinal numbers are almost all of Iranian origin, and in most cases identical with those in modern Persian. From the fourth upwards, they are formed by the addition of the termination *um* to the cardinal numbers, as in modern Persian. 'First' is expressed by *fartum*, Z. *fratema*, and by *nazdest*, Z. *nazdishta*, 'the nearest'; 'second' by which is pronounced *dod* by the Parsis, and also written, but which can only be identified with Chald. תִּנְיָן 'second' (see index, pag. 113), and is accordingly to be pronounced *tenê*; the Iranian equivalent is *datîgar*; 'third' by *satîgar*, Pers. سديگر; 'fourth' by *tasum* and *chchârum*, Pers. چهارم; 'fifth' by *panchum*, Pers. پنجم. Besides *um*, the termination *înu* = ين is also used for the formation of ordinals, e. g. *panchvînu*, 'the fifth'.

Distribrutives are formed by the addition of *kânu*, or *kânak*, Pers. گان, e. g. *do-kânak*, 'double', i. e. twin.

Multiplicatives are formed by the addition of *tâk*, e. g. *khaduk tâk*, 'one-fold'. The numeral adverbs are identical with those in Persian, being formed by the addition of بار.

d) Verbs.

The verbs are partly Semitic and partly Iranian. In the glossary, 104 very common verbs are enumerated, which are all of Semitic origin, and many of which we find in the inscriptions as well as in the books. Some of these verbs appear with, and others without, the prefix *ye, ya;* and as they are of the greatest importance for settling the true character of the Pahlavi language, I shall examine into their forms more minutely than might be expected in such an essay. First I shall point out those verbs, occurring in the inscriptions, which are readily identified with those of the MSS.

In the Sasanian Pahlavi, the following Semitic verbs are found: *a)* forms without the prefix, *ye*: *ramîtun* 'to throw', *shadîtun* 'to shoot', *hanakhtûn* 'to put', *vazlûn* 'to go', *hatîmûn* 'to complete (to fill)', *vakhdûn* 'to seize', *âstûn* 'to see', *khazîtun* 'to see', *sazîtun* 'to go', and *katab*, 'to write' (not used in this form in the books).

b) Forms with the prefix, *ye, ya*, which is now pronounced *je, ja*, by the Parsis, and is sometimes written *ze*, e. g. *zektalûn* (I. 40, 1.) which is however only a different orthography for *yektalûn* (Glos. 17, 3; see index, pag. 132. 238). The following forms, in the Sasanian Pahlavî, are readily identified with those of the books: *yahvûn* 'to be, to exist', *yekavîmûn* 'to be, to stand' (used as an auxiliary verb), *yakhmatûn* 'to come', *yektîbûn* 'to write', *yemanûn* 'to speak'; of *yamashkhûn*, 'to obtain', no equivalent is known in the MSS.; and *yekarîtun*, 'to call', is used without in the MSS., in the form, but the Sasanian reading is perhaps not correct. *c)* With the prefix *le*, we find *lekhadû*, 'to seize'.

In the Chaldæo-Pahlavî, there are the following Semitic verbs: *a)* without the prefix *ye*: הקאימו *haqâîmû*, 'to make stand, to place', Hifil of קום which is not used in this form in S.; נפל *napal* 'to fall' (see index, pag. 223, s. v. *vaflûnastan*), כרב *kadab* (= Chald. כְּתַב) *yektîbûn*, 'to write'; שדית *shadît* *shadîtûn*, 'to shoot'; רמית *ramît* *ramîtûn*, 'to throw'; בנית *banît*, 'to build, construct', used neither in S., nor in the books, Chald. בְּנָא. *b)* With the prefix *ye*: יהות *yehût* *yahvûn*, 'to be'; יאמזוד *yâmzûd*, 'to make reach, arrive', Hifil of מצא (see pag. 64). *c)* With the prefix *le*: לחדו *lekhadû*, 'to seize', from אחד (see pag. 56—57).

The Iranian verbs are not often used in the inscriptions, and only in the form of the past participle. The following occur in S.: *kalt*, *kaltî* (*kart*, *kartî*) کرده 'made'; *chîtî*, 'constructed'; *parmât* (*farmât*) فرموده 'ordered'; *napashtî* نپشته 'written'. In Ch. there is only one: *âûpadasht*, 'ordered' (see pag. 61).

Before discussing the forms of the Semitic verbs in Pahlavi, I have to make some remarks on the auxiliary verb which is used in all the Pahlavî dialects. In S. we find *hûman*, in Ch. הוין *havîn* (*hovîn*), and in P. *hûman*, used in connection with the verbs; and they all seem to be identical (see pag. 60). Their unusually frequent occurrence in Pahlavi, gives us, at the very outset, a hint that they must represent a very common word either in the Iranian, or in the Semitic languages. As it is used as an auxiliary verb, and none like it is discoverable in the Iranian languages, we can only trace it to a Semitic source; and indeed the form הוין in Chaldæo-Pahlavî, does not leave much doubt that it is some form of the verb הֲוָא, ܗܘܳܐ 'to be'. הוין may be pronounced *havîn*, or *hovîn*; in either case it is the plural masculine of the present participle of הֲוָא, which is in Chald. הָוֵין, in Syr. ܗܳܘܶܝܢ *hovên*; *hûman*, which may perhaps be better read *hômen*, is only another pronunciation of this, *m* being identical with *v*, as is really the case in Assyrian (see the index, pag. 193—194); this also throws some light on the termination [Pahlavi], to be discussed hereafter. That the plural *hovên*, *hômen*, was employed as the standard form, instead of the singular, is not surprising, as all the other verbal forms in Pahlavî, which are taken from the Semitic languages, appear in the plural, with the terminations *ûn*, *îtûn*. Another and stronger argument for the derivation of [Pahlavi] from הֲוָא, is the circumstance that both are used in the same way for the formation of tenses and moods. In Chaldee and Syriac, the imperfect and pluperfect are formed by the addition of הֲוָא, or ܗܘܳܐ, to the present participle and the perfect (the first tense of the Semitic languages), e. g. ܡܗܰܠܶܟ ܗܘܳܐ 'he went', lit. he was going; ܐܚܶܕ ܗܘܳܐ 'he had taken'. It is also occasionally used to express the conjunctive and conditional (see Hoffmann, Gram. Syr. pag. 336—337); and in modern Syriac it is more especially used in conditional sentences (see Nöldeke Gram. der neusyrischen Sprache, pag. 299—301). Now in Pahlavî, [Pahlavi] *hûman*, (*hômen*) is used exactly for the same purposes: *a)* for the formation of a real perfect tense, as in [Pahlavi], [Pahlavi] *kartu hûmanam* = کرده ام 'I have made'; *b)* in conditional sentences, as in [Pahlavi]

[Pahlavi]

[Pahlavi] *hat le lâ yahbûnt hûmenâi* .... *jinâk râmeshn deheshnyâ* .... *harvest ahvu-i ast-hûmand avu Airân-vêj fraj vazlûneshnyâ bud hûmenâi*, (Vend. 1, 3—4. Sp.) 'if I had not created a place of pleasantness, the whole world endowed with bodies would have gone forth to Irân-vêj'; comp. also the Hâjîâbâd inscriptions S. and Ch. lin. 9—10 (pag. 59—60). It is to be observed that [Pahlavi] is used in *both* clauses of the hypothetical sentences, just as ܗܘܳܐ in modern Syriac. — On this occassion I may also mention the word [Pahlavi] *âîtî* [Pahlavi] *aîtu*, 'it is', which is of very frequent use, and readily identified with the Chald. אִית (in the biblical Chald. אִיתַי, in the Talmud אִיתָא) Syr. ܐܝܬ, Hebr. יֵשׁ 'it is, exists'. Its negative is [Pahlavi] *lôît* 'there is not', Chald. לֵית, Syr, ܠܰܝܬ, Arab. لَيْسَ.

After these preliminary remarks, I proceed to state my views regarding the character of the Pahlavî verb. It is remarkable, at the very outset, that the commonest verbs are all of Semitic origin, including those expressing 'to go', 'to come', 'to be', 'to speak', 'to have', etc.; and this circumstance would lead us to expect that the Semitic element may also prevail over the Iranian, in the conjugation. This expectation is confirmed by the fact that, in the Sasanian version of the Hâjiâbâd inscription, all verbal terminations which might indicate an Iranian character, are entirely wanting. Moreover, it is from this inscription, as the oldest available record, that we must start, in order to arrive at the real character of the original Pahlavî conjugation.

All the Semitic verbs which are found in this, as well as the other inscriptions, and in the books, are easily recognized by the terminations *ûn*, S. and *îtûn*, S. *itun*, the *û* not being expressed in writing in the latter termination in S. As those which end in *îtûn*, form a separate class, I take them first. They are all traceable to the so-called ל"ה, or ל"א verbs in Hebrew and Chaldee, which is very remarkable. The list of verbs in the glossary contains the following which are of this kind, and of which the Semitic equivalents can be determined with certainty: *khavîtûn* (traditionally *anîtûn*), Syr. ܚܘܐ 'to know'; *khazîtûn* (trad. *azîtûn*), Chald. חֲזָא 'to see'; *karîtûn*, Chald. קְרָא 'to call'; *mahîtûn*, Chald. מְחָא 'to strike'; *manîtûn*, Chald. מְנָא 'to count'; *ramîtûn*, Chald. רְמָא 'to throw'; *sharîtûn*, Chald. שְׁרָא 'to open'; *zarîtûn*, 'to cultivate, to till', Heb. זָרָה 'to strew'; of the following, the Semitic equivalents have not been determined: *sarîtûn*, 'to cohabit'; *sazîtûn*, 'to go'; *shamîtûn*, 'to stitch'; *shakîtûn*, 'to take arrows to their aim', is probably miswritten for *shadîtûn*, Chald. שְׁדָא, as this is really used in Pahlavî books in the sense 'to shoot' (see pag. 52—53). In the Sasanian version of the Hâjiâbâd inscription, *ramîtun* and *shadîtun* belong to this class; and in the other inscriptions, *khazîtun* and *sazîtun* (see pag. 97).

The remainder of the Semitic verbs in Pahlavî, whether they prefix *ye*, or not, only add the termination *ûn* to the root, e. g. *yehabûn*, Chald. יְהַב 'to give'. The following have the prefix *ye, ya* (see pag. 97): *yekavîmûn* (trad. *jaknîmôn*) = יְקַיְמוּן, Chald. יְקִימוּן 'to stand'; *yektîbûn* = Chald. יִכְתְּבוּן 'to write'; *yektelûn*, *zaktalûn* (*jaktalûn*) = Chald. יִקְטְלוּן 'to kill'; *yâmtûn* = Chald. יְמַטוּן (Afel) 'to arrive, to obtain'; *yamlûn*, *yamrûn* = Chald. יֵאמְרוּן 'to speak'; *yemanenûn*, *yemalelûn* = Chald. יְמַלְלוּן (Pael) 'to speak'; *yakhsanû*, for *yakhsanûn* (trad. *dâsôn*) = Chald. יַחְסְנוּן 'to have, possess'; *yemîtûn* = Chald. יְמִיתוּן 'to kill'; *yansigûn* (trad. *josgûn*) = Heb. יַשִּׂיגוּן for יַנְשִׂיגוּן 'to take, to seize' (see index, pag. 135—136); *yehevûn*, *yahvûn* = Chald. יֶהֱווֹן 'to be'; *yâtûn*, *yâîtûn* = Chald. יֵיתוֹן (from אֲתָא) 'to come'; *yâîtîûn*, (trad. *jâîdgôn*) = Chald. יַיְתוֹן for יַיְתִין (from Afel אַיְתִי) 'to bring'; *yezbahûn* = Chald. יִזְבְּחוּן 'to sacrifice, worship'; *yeparhûn* (trad. *gaprhôn*) 'to wish, desire' = Chald. יִפְרְעוּן 'to avenge, retaliate', (comp. *parhônatan*, index, pag. 176).

All these verbs, in which *ye* (read by the Parsis, *je*, *ja*, *za*, or *ga*, and even *de*, as we shall see hereafter) is prefixed, and *ûn* is added, are easily recognized as third persons plural of the so-called imperfect (second tense in the Semitic languages), as the reader will have already noticed from the foregoing identifications. The termination of the 3[d] pers. pl. masc. of the imperfect, in Chaldee, is *ûn*, and in the ל״א verbs it is *ôn*. It is also very remarkable that none of the Pahlavî verbs, which can be traced to roots of the ל״א class, have the termination *îtûn* when *ye* is prefixed, although they always have it when the prefix is not used; comp. *yehevûn* and *ramîtûn*, from הֲוָא and רְמָא respectively.

Although the termination *ûn* does not offer any difficulty to the etymologist, when used with the prefix *ye*, the case is different when this prefix is wanting, or when the termination *îtûn* occurs instead of *ûn*. The latter suffix is joined to all classes of Semitic verbs, except those in ל״א (see pag. 100). I enumerate here, according to classes, some of the principal verbs to which it is joined, in the unmodified form Qal: 1) Regular verbs with three strong consonants: *katrûn*, 'to remain'; *tablûn*, *tabrûn*, תְּבַר 'to break'; *takrûn*, *taklûn*, תְּקַל 'to weigh'; *paskûn*, פְּסַק 'to cut'; *khalkûn* (trad. *arkôn*) 'to give', חֲלַק; *khalmûn* (trad. *armôn*) 'to sleep', חֲלַם; etc. 2) פ״א: *alpûn* (trad. *arpôn*), אֲלַף 'to learn'; *asrûn*, אֲסַר 'to bind'; sometimes the initial א is represented by ו, as in *vazlûn*, אֲזַל 'to go' (see index, pag. 230); *vakhdûn* (trad. *vâgôn*), אֲחַד 'to take, seize'. 3) פ״י: *yehabûn* (trad. *dâbôn*), יְהַב 'to give'; *yetîbûn*, יְתַב 'to sit' (this may be taken for the second tense 3 sg. יִתֵּב, pl. יִתְּבוּן). 4) פ״נ: *naflûn* (trad. *vaflôn*), נְפַל 'to fall'; *natrûn* (trad. *vatrôn*), נְטַר 'to guard'; *naksûn*, נְכַס 'to kill'. 5) פ״ע; the initial ע is generally represented by ו *v*, *û*, *o* (see index, pag. 231): *vâdûn*, עֲבַד 'to make', the ב being dropped; *varîkûn*, עֲרַק 'to flee'. 6) ע״ע: *khatatûn* (trad. *attôn*) חֲטַט 'to sew'. 7) ע״ו: *sâtûn*, 'to go', שׁוּט 'to turn away'; *lishûn* (trad. *rîshôn*), לוּשׁ 'to knead'; *kîlûn* (trad. *kadrôn*), כּוּל 'to measure'. 8) פ״א with ל״ה: *appûn*, אֲפָה 'to cook' 1).

Of the modified forms, the principal are Pael (intensive), Afel and Shaphel (both causative). Pael: *khavîtûn*, 'to know', חַוִּא; *khâîtûn*, 'to twist', חַיֵּט 'to sew'; *khalelûn* (trad. *alalôn*), 'to wash'; *zamarûn* (trad. *zamlôn*), זַמֵּר 'to sing'; and with the prefix *ye*: *yemalelûn* (trad. *jamnôn*), מַלֵּל 'to speak'; *yekavîmûn* (trad. *jaknîmôn* 'to stand', קַיֵּם for קוּם. 2) Afel: *ashkakhûn*,

1) For the ל״א class, see pag. 100. The modified forms of this class are however enumerated here again, along with the same modifications of the other classes, in order to set the Semitic character of the Pahlavî verb more clearly before the reader.

2) Although there can hardly be any doubt that *yekavîmûn* is to be traced to a Pael form, there is some difficulty as regards the meaning. The Pael קַיֵּם

אַשְׁכַּח 'to obtain'; *anakhtûn*, 'to put', אַנְחֵת; *hatîmûn* (trad. *atîmôn*), הַתֵּם from תְּמַם 'to complete' (see pag. 71); *haimenûn*, הֵימַן 'to believe' (see ind. pag. 47—48); *âîtûn*, אַיְתִי 'to bring', from אֲתָא; and with the prefix *ye*: *yâîtûn*, id.; *yemîtûn*, 'to kill', יְמִית; *yâmtûn*, 'to come', יִמְטֵי (יִמְטוּן). Shafel: *shochrûn*, *sochrûn*, 'to plunder, pillage', שַׁעְצַר.

There are some instances of other modifications of the Semitic verbs, besides those enumerated above. In 'to hear', which is traditionally read *vashmamôn*, I believed I recognized the Ithpeal, or Ithpael (both passive-reflexive forms of Peal, the unmodified verb, and Pael, the intensive form, respectively) of the root שְׁמַע 'to hear'; the Semitic form which underlies it, would be אִשְׁתְּמַע, or אִשְׁתַּמַּע, from which the *t* was dropped, and the initial א can be represented by ו (see index, pag. 228). The verb. 'to eat', which is traditionally read *vashtamôn*, I have explained as an Ishtafal (passive-reflexive form) of טְעַם 'to eat'; the original form אִשְׁתַּטְעַם being corrupted into אִשְׁטַעַם by dropping the first *t*, and א being again represented by ו. Both verbs can, however, be explained in another and, I think, more simple way, by means of the Assyrian, in which the Pael of שמע would be *yushamma* in the 3^d^, and *ushamma* in the 1st pers. sing.; and the Shafel of טעם would be *yushaṭam* and *ushaṭam* 1). The Pahlavî verbs *vashmamôn* and *vashtamôn* would thus correspond to the 3^d^ pers. pl. of the aorists (imperfects), *yushammûn*

---

has, in Chaldee, a causative meaning, 'to make firm, to promise, to swear, to preserve alive', while *yekavîmûn* has never any of these meanings, but is merely an equivalent of the Persian اِستادن 'to stand', and often used as an auxiliary verb. As this Pael is however of very frequent and extensive use in Chaldee, it is not surprising that the Persians, who spoke the Aramaic dialect which underlies the Pahlavî, confounded it with the Qal יְקוּם 'he stands', which would have been the proper equivalent for the Persian *istâdan;* for we should expect *yekûmûn*, instead of *yekavîmûn*.

1) See Oppert, Élémens de la grammaire assyrienne, 2d ed. pag. 61. 69.

and *yushtammûn*, when these have lost their initial *y*; this explanation appears to me preferable to the former, as it offers no phonetic difficulty.

Some verbs are difficult to class with the others, and deserve some special notice, as from the form in which they appear in Pahlavî, it cannot be at once determined whether they have a prefix or not. These are *dadrûn*, 'to bear, to take'; *dâbhûn*, 'to laugh'; *dazbamôn*, 'to wish, desire'; *madammûn*, 'to wish, to think, ponder'; *rapmamôn*, 'to bring'. *dadrûn* must be traced to Chald. דְּרָא 'to carry' (see index, pag. 103); if the first letter be *da*, according to tradition, we could only explain it as the Chaldee relative דִּי, דְּ, and the verb would thus correspond to דְּדָרֵי 'who bears, or carries'; but this is a phrase and not a verbal form; and as the prefix must generally be read *ye*, as is clearly proved from the inscriptions, it will be better to do so in this case, and read *yadrûn* which is then a form like *yâîtûn*. 'to laugh', cannot be explained in any way, if we read it *dâbhôn*, according to tradition; it can be derived from Chald. חוּךְ 'to laugh', which is frequently used in the imperfect of Pael יְחַיֵּךְ which stands for יְחַוֵּךְ, in the same way as יְקַיֵּם does for יְקוּם (comp. *yekavîmûn*); I propose therefore to read *yekhabkhûn* = יְחַיְּחוּן for יְחַוְּחוּן; the substitution of *b* for *v* is not surprising, and the change of the final *k* into *kh* need be no difficulty, as they sometimes interchange in the Semitic languages (comp. Heb. מחר and מכר). 'to wish', cannot be traced to any Semitic root, if we adhere to the traditional reading *dazbamôn*; I propose to read it *yezbamûn*, and trace it to a root צבם which appears to be identical with צבא 'to wish'. In *madammûn*, the participial prefix *ma* may perhaps be recognized, but I am not certain about it; this verb must be derived from דַּמֵּה 'to think, imagine'. In , traditionally read *rapmamôn*, we have probably an Assyrian optative form, with the prefix *le*; I read it *lipammûn* = *libammûn* (see index, pag. 193—194, see more about *le* further on).

Having examined all the Semitic verbs in Pahlavî, which can be of any importance in deciding the question as to the form in which they appear, I proceed to state my conclusions regarding the termination *ûn*. As the reader will have seen, it is used in various ways: *a)* with the prefix *ye*; *b)* without it; *c)* preceded by *ît*, forming *îtûn*; *d)* with the prefixes *ma* and *le*. Regarding the forms with the prefix *ye*, there cannot be the slightest doubt (as has been already remarked) that they are in the 3d pers. pl. masc. of the second Semitic tense, the so-called imperfect, aorist, or future, the termination of which 3d pers. pl. is *ûn*, *ôn*, in the Chaldee, Syriac and Mandæan dialects; they agree in almost every particular with the respective Chaldee forms, as is evident from the instances quoted above (pag. 101).

It is more difficult to determine, to which Semitic form we have to trace the other verbs ending in *ûn*, but without the prefix *ye*. The most natural supposition is that they represent the 3d pers. pl. masc. of the first Semitic tense, the so-called perfect, or preterit; but the circumstance that its termination is generally *û* in the Aramaic languages, and only rarely *ûn*, is not very favorable to this opinion. As no other suitable tense, or form, can be found, I think they must also be traced to the second tense (the imperfect) with the omission of the prefix *ye*. It is true that such an omission is unusual in the Semitic languages, but some instances of it occur in the Assyrian (Oppert, Gram. assyr. preface pag. XX). Some weight may also be attached to the fact, that the second tense, with the prefixes, is exclusively used in the Assyrian versions of the Persian inscriptions (see the list of verbs in Oppert l. c. pag. 47—49), as well as in the historical records of Babylon and Niniveh; no certain traces of the first tense having been as yet discovered. A further proof in favor of the opinion I have advanced, is afforded by the two verbs *âîtûn* and *yâîtîûn*, 'to bring', the former of which is merely an abbreviation of the latter, by the omission of the prefix *ye*; this is evident from its termination being *ûn*, and not *îtûn*, for its root אֲתָא 'to come', is of the ל״א class, which in Pahlavî take the termination *ûn* only when they have the prefix *ye*, but when without that prefix, they take the termination *îtûn* (see above, pag. 101).

Now arises the question, how are the forms in *îtûn* to be explained? I took them at first for the 2[d] pers. pl. masc. of the first tense, which in Chaldee, ends in *êtûn*, *îtûn* (סְגִיתוּן, גְּלִיתוּן); but I cannot uphold this view, as it would be very strange, if the verbs in ל״א were used in the 3[d] pers. pl. masc. of the second tense, when preceded by the prefix *ye*, and in the 2[d] pers. pl. masc. of the first tense, when not preceded by it. As we find these verbs in Chaldæo-Pahlavî, ending only in *ît*, without the *ûn*, e. g. *shadît*, *ramît*, *banît*, and construed like passive participles, we may not be wrong, if we take them as such also in Sasanian Pahlavî. Now the past participles of the verbs ל״א, in the unmodified form in Chaldee, end in *î*, *ê*, in the masc. sing., and in *yâ* in the fem. sing., which latter becomes *yat* in the *status constructus*, and *îtâ* in the *status emphaticus*; in Syriac, the masc. sing. is *î*, the fem. sing. *ît* in the stat. constr., and *îtô* in the stat. emph.; in Assyrian, the masc. is *û*, the fem. *it*, e. g. *banit* (see Oppert, Gram. assyr. pag. 87). Thus the Chaldæo-Pahlavî *ramît*, *shadît*, *banît* correspond exactly to the Syriac forms ܪܡܝܬ *r'mît*, ܫܕܝܬ *sh'dît*, ܒܢܝܬ *b'nît*, which are feminines of the past participles, in the *status constructus*, of the roots ܪܡܐ, ܫܕܐ, ܒܢܐ; in Chaldee, the corresponding forms are רְמִית, שְׁדִית, בְּנִית, where *yat* is used instead of *ît*. If we now proceed to explain the Pahlavî verbal forms ending in *îtûn* (in Sasanian Pahlavî *ître*, *îtun*, or *îtan*) in the same way, as we are fully justified in doing, the final syllable *ûn* appears to offer some difficulty; but this is solved by reference to Assyrian, in which there is a plural termination *ûn*, used sometimes with participles, e. g. מְצַבְּתוּן 'the captives' (Oppert, Gram. assyr. pag. 26). The verbal forms in *îtûn*, according to this investigation, are plurals of passive participles in the feminine gender, of verbs of the ל״א class. That they are taken from the Semitic languages in the plural form, is not surprising, as the other verbal forms appear also in the plural.

In the same manner, the final *ûn* in *madammûn*, can be explained, if the prefix *ma* be taken as an indication of the participle, as it may be; in that case, however, *madammûn* must be derived from a root דמה of the ל״ה class, and ought to end in *îtûn*; but this difficulty may be removed, by taking it as the plur. masc. with the loss of י before *ûn*, as occurs in the 3ᵈ pers. pl. masc. of the second tense.

The explanation of the final *ûn* in *libammûn* (*rupammûn*) 'to bring' (see index, pag. 193—194) is simple enough. The prefix *l* is well known in Assyrian, as forming optatives with the terminations of the second tense (see Oppert, Gramm. assyr. pag. 51—52); لِ *li* occurs also in Arabic to form imperatives of the 3ᵈ person, as in لِيَكْتُبْ 'let him write', (it is not to be confounded with لَ *la* before the emphatic mood ending in *anna*); in the Chaldaic portions of the Old Testament, לְ is frequently prefixed to הֲוָא with the terminations of the second tense, as in לֶהֱוֺן, לֶהֱוֵא, in the sense of an optative, precative, imperative, or simple future (see Dan. 2, 20. 28. 41. 43. 3, 18. etc.). In the Chaldæo-Pahlavî of the Hâjîâbâd inscription, there is also להוינד *le-havînd* (see pag. 58).

From the preceding remarks, the reader will see that the Semitic verbs in Pahlavî are partly passive participles, and partly 3ᵈ persons of the second tense, but in either case always in the plural. Now in this shape, they were certainly not much adapted to the requirements of those who used the language, as the persons have to be expressed in one way or other. In the Hâjîâbâd inscription, the oldest record of the Sasanian Pahlavî, in which verbs are found, they occur in the manner described, without any suffix denoting the person; the only terminations observable being *ûn* and *îtun* which have been already described.

In the Chaldæo-Pahlavî version of the same inscription, there is in most cases a *t*, *d*, or *dî* at the end of the Semitic verbs, which it will be difficult to explain from the Semitic languages, except in *ramît*, *shadît*, *banît* (see pag. 106) and perhaps *napalt*. In the last, נפלת lin. 8, the *t* cannot be the termination of the 1ˢᵗ pers. sing. of the first tense, which is נִפְלֵת in Chaldee, as the first person is not used in the sentence; but it might be the 3ᵈ pers. sing. fem. נִפְלַת, or the *status constructus* of the feminine participle of the active voice נָפְלַת; the latter interpretation is preferable, as *ramît*, etc. clearly show that feminine participles were really used in this dialect. The connection with להוינד, which is the *verbum finitum*, shows that it is a participle, as the verb הֲוָא 'to be', is very frequently used, with the active participle, to form present and past tenses, for instance, חָזֵה הֲוַיְתָ 'thou wast seeing'; the verbal form נפלת להוינד would be נָפְלָא לְהֱוֵא in Chaldee. Another participal form is כדב lin. 11. 14. = Chald. כָּתֵב 'writing'.

The other Semitic verbs in Chaldæo-Pahlavî, which have a final *t*, or *d*, cannot be explained as Semitic participles, as regards their form; we find, for instance, הקאימות *haqâîmût* (*haqâîmûd*, lin. 12), יאמזוד *yâmzûd* and יהות *yehût*. הקאימות may be traced to the 3ᵈ pers. pl. of the first tense, Heb. הֵקִימוּ, Chald. אֲקִימוּ; יאמזוד may be traced to יַמְטוּ, the 3ᵈ pers. plur. of the so-called *futurum apocopatum* of the Afel of מְטָא 'to come'; and יהות may be traced to יְהוּ, the 3ᵈ pers. sg. of the fut. apoc. of הֲוָא 'to be'; the final *t*, or *d*, must be an Iranian termination, in these verbs, but that it was not originally wanted, is shown by *haqâîmû* occurring without it, in the Pâî-Kûlî inscription 26, 3. and also by שדיו *shadyû* in Hâj. Ch. lin. 13. If we trace this termination to the Iranian languages, it must be either the termination of the past participle, or that of the 3ᵈ pers. sing. of the present, or imperfect tense In Hâj. Ch. lin. 7. ('the feet were placed in this cave'), the construction requires a past participle as *haqâîmût* stands in parallel with *ramît*; but in lin. 12, a 3ᵈ pers. pl. of the conjunctive, or imperative, is wanted, and here the *d* in *haqâîmûd* is evidently the sign of a 3ᵈ pers. but is probably superfluous, as it is wanting in the parallel word *shadyû*. In lin. 9, *yehût* must be a past participle; but in lin. 8, it is a 3ᵈ pers. sing., according to the context, and so is *yâmzûd* in lin. 14; the final *t*, or *d*, in these last two cases, must therefore be the characteristic of the 3ᵈ pers. sing. Instead of *t*, or *d*, we sometimes find *dî* = Zand *tî*, as the characteristic of the 3ᵈ pers. sing., e. g. *havîndî*.

Now the addition of Iranian terminations to inflected Semitic verbs, looks rather strange, but it is nevertheless a fact, and finds its complete analogy and explanation in Assyrian, as will be shown hereafter. This addition forms one of the characteristics of the Sasanian Pahlavî and occurs throughout the MSS. and frequently in the inscriptions, except in the

Sasanian version of the Hâjîâbâd inscription. The reader will however have learned, from the third section of this essay, that these terminations are not always added, even in the later inscriptions. Thus, for instance, they are never added to *yahvûn* (*yehevûn*, N. Raj. 6. 11., 13. 15. P. K. 17, 5. 18, 2. N. Rust. 53. 58. 60); other instances of this omission are [illegible] *yahmatûn* (N. Raj. 22. N. Rust. 28; but *yahmatûnt* in N. Raj. 21), [illegible] *yektîbûn* (N. Raj. 25), [illegible] *vakhdûn* (P. K. 3, 5), [illegible] *yekhshûn* (P. K. 7, 5) and [illegible] *yemanûn* (N. Raj. 18); to the auxiliary verb [illegible] *hûman* (see pag. 98), the termination of the 3[d] pers. is never added, as we always find [illegible] for the [illegible] *hûm-anad* of the MSS. (N. Raj. 6. 19. P. K. 22, 1); but we find it with the characteristic *m* of the 1st pers., forming [illegible] *hûmanam* = [illegible] (N. Raj. 4. 11. 12. 13. 27. 28. 29. 31).

The Iranian terminations are thus seen to be entirely wanting in the oldest of the known Sasanian inscriptions containing verbs, and were only gradually and optionally used in the subsequent inscriptions of the third century A. D.; these facts clearly indicate that these terminations did not form part of the original Pahlavî, which Ardeshîr Bâbegân made the official language of Persia. It is true that they are never wanting in the MSS., as they have been handed down to us, and it is chiefly on this account, that the original Pahlavî has been declared to have been an Iranian language; but this opinion is no longer tenable, since we find there was a period when these Iranian terminations were not used. According to the foregoing investigation, the original state of the verbal conjugation in Pahlavî, seems to have been as follows: Semitic verbs were used instead of Iranian ones, and represented, for the most part, the 3[d] pers. pl. masc. of the second tense, the so-called Assyrian aorist, which tense prevailed over all others in the ancient languages of Babylon and Niniveh; some verbs however (those traceable to roots of the so-called ל״ה and ל״א classes) were used in the past participle pl. fem. These forms were used, without regard to their grammatical meaning, to express only the verbal idea. That the Iranians chose these forms, and no others, may be explained by the supposition that they were most frequently used in that Aramaic dialect, from which Pahlavî arose. The persons of the verb were expressed by suffixes joined to a particle (generally *âp* = אף), which was placed at the beginning of the sentence; and for the expression of tenses and moods, the auxiliary verb ܗܘܡܢ *hûman* = [Pahlavi] was used (see pag. 99). But this way of conjugating the verb, was soon found very insufficient; and as the Persians began to read the Iranian equivalents for the Semitic words (see pag. 38), they found it convenient to add the Iranian terminations; and hence the conjugation assumed an Iranian appearance.

The Pahlavî of the MSS. distinguishes four moods, viz. indicative, conjunctive, conditional and imperative. The indicative has a present tense, a first preterit and a second preterit; the conjunctive has a present tense and a preterit; and the conditional has two forms, one of which is a preterit.

Indicative. The terminations of the present tense are like those in modern Persian, viz. 1st sing. *am* = Z. *âmi*, pl. *îm* = Z. opt. *aêma;* 2d sing. ي *ai* = Z. ind. *ahi, âi,* pl. *ît, ad* = Z. opt. *aêta,* ind. *ati;* 3d sing. *ît, êt* = Z. opt. *aêta*, pl. [Pahlavi] *and* = Z. ind. *anti*. Ex. [Pahlavi] *vâdûnam*, 'I make', [Pahlavi] *vâdûnai,* [Pahlavi] *vâdûnêt;* [Pahlavi] *vâdûnîm,* [Pahlavi] *vâdûnît,* [Pahlavi] *vâdûnand.* The first preterit is nothing but the past participle[1]), which is used either with, or without, the final [Pahlavi] *u*, or [Pahlavi] = ؤ *î* in S. (comp. *âstûndî*): Ex. [Pahlavi] *vâdûnt*, 'he made'; a final *d* is also used instead of *t* (comp. N. Raj. 18. 19. 20. 21, see pag. 69—70); when necessary, the persons are expressed by pronominal suffixes joined to [Pahlavi] *âp*, or to some other particle (see above): Ex. [Pahlavi] [Pahlavi] *âpmân vâdûnt*, 'we made' (comp. N. Raj. 20. 21. 22. 24, see pag. 70—71). The second preterit is formed by the auxiliary verb [Pahlavi] *hûman* (see pag. 99), or [Pahlavi] *yekavîmûn*, to which the terminations of the present tense are added; it is used both actively and passively: Ex. [Pahlavi] [Pahlavi] *vazlûnt yekavîmûnêt*, 'he has gone', [Pahlavi] [Pahlavi]

---

1) I have shown this in my review of Spiegel's Pârsî grammar, in the Göttinger Gelehrte Anzeigen of 1853, pag. 196—197.

kartu hûmanam, 'I have made' (comp. *kaltî hûmanam*, N. Raj., see pag. 72—74). Instead of *hûman*, *havîtun*, (the past part. pl. fem., see pag. 106) seems to have been also used in the inscriptions, thus in N. Rust. 2. we find *kaltî havîtun*, which has probably a passive meaning, 'he was made'. *yekavîmûnt* is also found, in N. Rust. 8, in connection with a past participle ; supplying for the missing letter we obtain *nipishtî yekavîmûnt*, 'he has written', or 'it has been written'. A separate future tense is wanting; the present tense and the conjunctive being used to express it, as is the case in Zand and Vedic Sanscrit; and sometimes = به, or *hamâi*, is prefixed to a verb with a future meaning.

Conjunctive. The only terminations which occur are 2ᵈ sing. *êsh*, (*sh*); 3ᵈ sing. *ât*, pl. *ând*, *ênd*, *yen*. These are all remnants of the ancient Iranian conjugation, as shown by the old-Persian and Zand; *êsh*, *îsh* is evidently the 2ᵈ sing. opt. mid. in Z. *aêsha; ât* is the 3ᵈ sing. conj. pres. act.; *ând* the 3ᵈ pl. conj. pres. act. *âoñti* = *ânti*; *înd* the 3ᵈ pl. opt. mid. *yañta;* and *yen* the 3ᵈ pl. opt. act. *ayen*, *yen*. Ex. *vâdûnêsh*, *vâdûnyen*, etc. There is also a perfect of the conjunctive in use, which is formed by the auxiliary verb *hûman*, or *yekavîmûn*, with the terminations of the conjunctive, as *hûmandt*, etc. added to the past participle of the verb.

Imperative. The 1ˢᵗ sing. ends in *âni*, just as in Zand, and appears to be also used for the plural; the 2ᵈ sing. is merely the crude form of the verb, as *vâdûn;* the 2ᵈ pl. ends in *ît*, which must be traced to the 2ᵈ pl. opt. *aêta*.

Conditional. This mood is formed by adding , , *hûmandi*, without any personal terminations, to the past participle. In the Sasanian inscriptions also, *hûman* is used to express this mood; see pag. 59—60.

Participles. The present participle ends in *ân* = Z. *añt*; and the past participle ends in *tu*, S. *tî* = Z. *ta*. The infinitive is formed by the suffix *tanu* (probably for *tani*) = old-Pers. *tanaiy*, modern Pers. تن, دن.

The forms ending in *eshnu*, *eshnyâ*, or *eshnîh*, deserve special notice; they are chiefly used in the sense of a Latin future participle passive in *andus*, *endus*, as *vâdûneshnu*, 'it is to be done'; but they are also used in the sense of a 3d pers. of the imperative, or optative, e. g. *setâyeshnîh*, 'let him praise' (Vend. 19, 73.), and likewise abstract nouns, e. g. *gubeshnu*, 'speaking, speech'.

The origin of these terminations, which are applied equally to Semitic and Iranian verbs, is difficult to ascertain; see my remarks on them in the Zand-Pahl.-Gloss. pag. XXVIII.

The causative is formed by adding the termination *în* to the crude forms; this is probably traceable to a nominal suffix *ayana* derived from the old causal in *aya*.

The passive voice is formed like the 2d preterit, by means of the auxiliary verbs *hûman* and *yekavîmûn*, and can hardly be distinguished from the active; this is not to be wondered at, as the essential part of both preterits is the past participle (see above, pag. 110).

e) Remarks on some suffixes.

There are some suffixes in Pahlavî which deserve special notice, as they appear to be of Semitic origin.

1. *man*, S. (see pag. 44—45). This suffix is only found at the end of Semitic words of various classes, such as nouns, pronouns, verbs and adverbs. Its origin cannot therefore be always the same. In the adverbs *tamman*, S. 'there', and *letamman*, 'here', it clearly corresponds to the syllable *mân* in Chaldee, as we recognize , without any change in תַּמָּן *tammân*, 'there', לְתַמָּן *letammân*, 'thither'. Its occurrence in the auxiliary verb *hûman*, S. ,

has been already explained (pag. 98); it is there a contraction of *vain,* and *hûman* stands for an original *hôvain.* But it is most frequently found at the end of nouns, especially those which signify parts of the body, e. g. *rôêshman,* 'head'; *shârman,* 'hair'; *aînman,* 'eye'; *anapman,* *anamman* (אנף) 'face'; *pumman,* 'mouth'; *yadman,* 'hand'; *aôjtapman,* 'finger'; *ragalman,* 'foot'; *lebabman,* 'heart'; *garûjadman,* 'belly'; etc. Two of these words occur in both versions of the Hâjîâbâd inscription, viz. = S. *lagalman* and Ch. נגרין *nagarîn,* and = S. *yadman* and Ch. ידא *yadâ.* It is remarkable that S. *lagalman* should be rendered by Ch. נגרין = רגרין, which is evidently a plural form; but the suffix *man* can also be explained, without difficulty, as a plural termination, *vân,* of the Chaldee, *m* and *v* always interchanging in Assyrian (see index, pag. 193—194); for Chaldee nouns whose singular ends in *ût,* stat. absol. *û,* form their plural stat. absol. in *vân,* e. g. מַלְכוּת 'empire', stat. absol. מַלְכוּ pl. מַלְכְוָן *malkvân.* This termination *vân,* which clearly presupposes a singular in *u,* is however not confined to feminine abstract nouns in *ût,* but is also used as an optional plural form of other nouns, thus we have נְהַר 'a river', pl. נַהֲרִין and נַהַרְוָן *naharvân;* אִזְמֵל 'a knife', pl. אִזְמְלִין and אִזְמַלְוָן *izmalvân;* סוּס 'a horse', pl. סוּסִין and סוּסְוָן *sûsvân;* אָת 'a sign, miracle', pl. אָתִין and אָתְוָן *atvân;* etc. Many of the nouns which take the suffix *man,* are the names of such parts of the body as exist in a duality, or plurality, such as the hands, feet, eyes, hair and nose (the two nostrils, comp. Heb. אַפַּיִם); some however are only single, such as the head and mouth; while another class of these nouns can be either singular or plural, such as *barman,* 'son', *bartman,* 'daughter', *nêshman,* 'wife', *khâtman,* 'sister'; but the use of the plural of these words can be easily accounted for, as it is customary to speak of family relationships in a collective form, such as sons, daughters, sisters and (where polygamy is practised) wives. It is more difficult to account for the plural form of some other words, such as *napshman,* 'self, himself'. In such cases the old termination *vân* was perhaps confounded with the suffix *ân*, which forms abstract and concrete nouns in Chaldee. In the pronouns and , *man* is probably also traceable to a plural termination, as they may stand for *denvân* and *ulvân*, which presuppose singulars like *denût* and *ulût*; the form, sing. masc. *ullu*, fem. *ullât*, 'that one', occurs in Assyrian. The preposition *levatman*, 'with', was originally an abstract noun לְוָת, from לְוָא 'to join', and may have been used in the plural, as is the case with several prepositions which were originally nouns, e. g. Chald. קֳדָם 'before', in קֳדָמֵיכוֹן 'before you', where קֳדָמֵי is in the *status constructus* pl. m.; Chald. בַּתְרֵי, בָּתַר 'after' (comp. Heb. אַחֲרֵי from אַחַר); etc. In *lanman*, 'we, ours', *man* appears to stand for *hûman*, being omitted from *lan-hûman*, 'belonging to us', i. e. 'ours', Chald. לָן הָוַיִן, or לָן הָוָן; in *lî-ûman* (trad. *ragôman*) 'mine', we have a similar form, almost unaltered.

The results of this investigation are that *man* is traceable: *a)* to a suffix *ân* preceded by a radical *m* which is doubled, as in ; *b)* to the Chaldee plural termination *vân*, or the nominal termination *ân*; *c)* to the part. act. pl. masc. *hûman*, *hôman* = Syr. *hôvên* 'being, existing, belonging'. The use of plural terminations is not surprising, as verbal forms were also received into Pahlavî in the plural; these terminations had, for the most part, lost their meaning, when the so-called Huzvâresh was formed.

2. *yâ*, or *îh*. This suffix, which has not been discovered in the inscriptions, is found at the end of Iranian as well as Semitic words, and does not appear to have always had the same origin. In Semitic words, it is sometimes only a variant of the *â*, in which so many Semitic words end in Pahlavî, and which is the termination of the *status emphaticus* in the singular; thus represents only בִּשְׂרָא 'flesh', and stands for *besrâ*, as is evident from Ibn Muqaffa's quotation (see pag. 38). Now the question arises, is only an orthographical variety of , or was it originally a different termination, the proper meaning of which is lost? I think the latter must be the case, for that was really pronounced *yâ*, is clearly proved by the word *meyâ*, 'water', which

could not be explained if read in any other way. It is, in my opinion, the *status emphaticus* of the plural, as Chald. מַלְכַיָּא 'the kings', from מַלְכָּא 'the king'. In some of the words which have this termination, it can be easily explained as a plural form, e. g. *shemayâ*, or *shemayyâ* (trad. *shamkâ*) = שְׁמַיָּא 'heaven', which is always used in the plural; also in *hunayâ*, for *hudnayyâ* = אוּדְנַיָּא 'ears', in *menayâ*, *melayâ* (trad. *môdâ*) = מִלַּיָּא 'words, speech', and in other words, the plural form can be easily accounted for, as these terms are perhaps more frequently used in the plural than in the singular. But there are some words with this termination, which are essentially singular in their meaning, such as *shemsyâ* = שִׁמְשָׁא 'the sun', *kamryâ*, 'the moon' (which is unknown in Chaldee, but exists in the Arabic قَمَر), and these must stand for *shemsâ* and *kamrâ;* the plural form being simply misapplied, as we have seen is sometimes the case with the termination *man.* It is more difficult to explain, when it is added to Iranian, or Semitic words, to form abstract nouns, as in 'knowledge, wisdom', which is read *dânâgî*, from *dânâk*, 'wise'; here is best identified with the modern Persian abstract suffix *î*. In the Sasanian inscriptions, some abstract nouns in *î* actually occur, as , *pâtakhshatrî* = پادشاهی, but none in *yâ*; whether *hî*, in *tagalâhî*, 'edict, order', be identical, is doubtful. In *ashbâryâ*, or *asbâryâ*, 'assisting, assistance', can be easily explained as the termination of a Semitic infinitive, which is an abstract noun; for *yâ* is really used, in the Mandæan dialect, to form the infinitives of the modified verbs, and to such a form (the Afel of סְבַר), *asbaryâ* is to be traced (see the index, pag. 55, s. v. *aiabârî*). With regard to the question whether this suffix can be traced to an Aryan, or to a Semitic source, when used for forming abstract nouns, it must be remarked that there is no abstract suffix *yâ*, either in Sanscrit, or Zand, and it is therefore not safe to trace it to an Aryan origin; but it is probably the Semitic infinitive termination *yâ* which has been just described. Alongside this termination there must also have been a form in *î*, or *é*; this we find to be the case in the Chaldaic dialects of the Talmud and the Targums, where there are infinitives (abstract nouns) in *ê*, as סיועי 'to help, helping', אנוחי *anûkhê*, 'to place, placing'; and such forms have been preserved in modern Syriac (see Noeldeke, Gram. der neusyr. Sprache, pag. 214).

3. used chiefly for the formation of adverbs from nouns. This suffix is generally read *îhâ*, and explained as an old Zand instrumental of nouns ending in *aṇh*; but this is quite illusory, and cannot be accounted for in any reasonable way. It is probably of Semitic origin, and may be identical with the Assyrian termination *ish*, which forms adverbs from nouns (see Zand-Pahl. Gl. pag. XXVII), and with the Syriac termination *ôît* (for *âish*), used for the same purpose (see the index, pag. 53). I propose reading it *yîsh*, *yêsh*, comp. Heb. יֵשׁ 'it is, exists'; it is true, this word occurs, in Pahlavî in its Chaldee form *aît*, but the original *sh* may have been preserved, when the word was used as a termination. Words formed with this suffix, such as and , may be thus analysed: *dânâk-yêsh*, 'being wise, or as a wise man', i. e. 'wisely'; and *vanâskâr-yêsh*, 'being a sinner, or as a sinner', i. e. 'sinfully'.

4. , , *shn*, *shnu* (*shni*). This suffix, which has been already mentioned (pag. 112), cannot be explained from any Semitic, or Aryan language. It is probably of Turanian origin, as it is found in the second class of the Achæmenian cuneiform inscriptions (see the Zand-Pahl. Gl. pag. XXVIII). It is principally used for forming abstract nouns, and seems to be still preserved in the modern Persian termination *ish*.

5. *hûmand* is a suffix used to form adjectives, and is still preserved in modern Persian, e. g. برومند, although it is generally there shortened to *mand* (for *ûmand*). It is usually traced to the Aryan suffix *mant* which, when added to substantives, gives the same adjectival meaning as *hûmand*; but this derivation does not explain the initial *hû*. I take it, unhesitatingly, as identical with the auxiliary verb *hûman* +

participal suffix ڌ *d*, and this, as we have seen, is of Semitic origin (see pag. 98).

6. ﻭ *ak*, ﺩﻭ *îk*, ﻭﺍ *ûk*. This final ﻭ is found at the end of many words, and is represented in Persian by ﻩ *h*, if preceded by a short vowel, as in ماده *mâdah* = *mâtak*, or is omitted when preceded by a long vowel, as in دانا *dânâ* = *dânâk*. The Parsis do not pronounce the *k*, and consider it superfluous. It is sometimes of Aryan, and sometimes of Semitic origin. When preceded by short *a*, and represented by ﻩ in modern Persian, it is the old Aryan suffix *ka;* this is clear from = بنده = old-Pers. *bandaka*, 'servant'; but when there is neither *k* in the ancient, nor ﻩ in modern Persian, the final ﻭ is of Semitic origin, e. g. *Pârsîk* = پارسی = old-Pers. *Pârsâ*, 'a Persian'; here it is the guttural which is so frequent in Assyrian words, as a final after vowels, see the Zand-Pahl. Gl. pag. XXVII. The final *îk* often corresponds to the termination *î*, or *ai*, in the Semitic languages, by which *nomina gentilicia* are formed, e. g. Heb. פַּרְסִי 'a Persian', יִשְׂרְאֵלִי 'an Israelite', עַרְבִי 'an Arab'; Assyr. *Pârsai*, Chald. פַּרְסִי or פַּרְסַי 'a Persian'. As the form پارسی is identical with these Semitic expressions, but not with the old-Persian *Pârsa*, the Semitic origin of the *î* is clear enough. The so-called یای وحدة *ê*, which is found in Pahlavi and modern Persian, is probably identical with it.

f) Particles.

The most common particles are of Semitic origin. In the Sasanian inscriptions, Iranian particles are very rare, only one certain instance having been noticed, viz. (Hâj. S. 10) = بیرون 'outside, out, forth'; a second instance may be (N. Raj. 22) = چگونه 'how', but this reading is less certain. In the scanty fragments of the Chaldæo-Pahlavi, no trace of an Iranian particle has been found.

1. Adverbs. In the inscriptions are the following: S. *tamman*, Ch. id., 'there' = , Chald. תַּמָּן; S. *âdîn*, Ch. id.,

'then' = , Chald. אֱדַיִן (see ind. pag. 90); S. *akhar*, 'after, afterwards' = , Heb. Assyr. אַחַר; S. *âmat*, Ch. id., 'when, as' = , Mandæan עמאת (see ind. pag. 47); S. *balâ*, Ch. לברא ,ברא 'out, out of' = *barâ*, Chald. לְבָרָא ,בָּרָא; S. *lûînî*, 'before' = , Chald. לְעֵינֵי 'before the eyes'; Ch. קדמתמן 'before' = Chald. קֳדָמַת (before suffixes); S. *lâ*, Ch. id., 'not' = , Chald. לָא; S. , Ch. הוף (for הווף) 'dont' = Assyr. אי (see pag. 62—63); S. *âp* = , Chald. אַף, to which the pronominal suffixes are joined, see pag. 51—52. In the MSS., there are the following adverbs of Semitic origin, besides those already mentioned: *letamman*, 'here', Chald. לְתַמָּן; *lâlâ*, 'upwards', Chald. לְעֵילָא; *lâkhvâr* (trad. *rânâr* and *rakhâr*) 'back, away', Chald. לְאָחוֹר; *aêmat* (trad. *admat*) 'how, when', Syr. أَمْثَمْ 'when'?; *admandîn*, 'in this manner' (see ind. pag. 45—46); *adûdûnak*, 'in this manner '(see ind. pag. 49); *kûn*, 'now', Chald. כְּעַן; *al*, 'dont', Heb. אַל (not found in Chaldee). There were originally very few Iranian adverbs; one was probably 'how', which is traditionally pronounced *chasûn*, but is better read *chigûn;* *aîtûn*, 'thus, now', is identical with ايدون, but its Iranian origin is doubtful (see index, pag. 50).

2. Prepositions. In the inscriptions are the following: S. *le*, 'to, in order to' (Hâj. S. 7), in Ch. the sign of the acc. (see pag. 57), Chald. לְ; S. *ûl, val*, Ch. *kal* = , 'to, for', Chald. עַל (see ind. pag. 226); S. *madam* = 'on'; S. *pavan* = 'in', Ch. *patan*, or *pavîn* (see ind. pag. 180); S. *min* = 'from', Chald. מִן, Ch. appears to have בְּ 'in', in *bîsh* (Hâj. Ch. 7). In the MSS. there are the following additional prepositions: *barâ*, 'without', Chald. בָּרָא (see adverbs); *yîn* (trad. *dayen*) 'in', comp. Assyr. *in;* *levatman*, 'with', Chald. לְוָת; *vad*, 'till, until', Chald. עַד (see ind. pag. 222—223): *bâtar*, 'after', Chald. בָּתַר. One preposition of Iranian

origin is *javît* (Z. *yûta*), Pers. جُز 'except'; and *râi* is a post-position, see ind. pag. 195—196.

3. Conjunctions. In the inscriptions are the following: S. *âîk*, Ch. id., 'that' (also the adverb 'where') = (see ind. pag. 87—88); S. *hat*, 'if' = , Arab. حتّى, Ch. *âk*; S. *û*, Ch. id., 'and' = , Chald. וְ; *meman*, 'for'. In the MSS. there are the following additional conjunctions: *ayûp*, 'or', comp. Heb. Chald. אוֹ (see ind. pag. 48—49); *vadnâ*, 'but, unless', עַד־לָא. Of very frequent use is *ch* appended to words, in the sense of 'also, even'; it is the ancient Aryan enclitic *cha*.

g) Some remarks on the construction of sentences.

The arrangement of the words in a Pahlavî sentence has more of an Aryan than a Semitic appearance. The genitive is, chiefly in titles, placed before the noun with which it is connected, e. g. *malkân malkâ*, 'regum rex'; *magûpatân magûpat*, 'the mobed of the mobeds', i. e. 'the chief mobed'; and this is never the case in the Semitic languages; but it is also often placed after the other noun, in which case, the *idhâfat* intervenes in the MSS., but not in the inscriptions. The adjectives follow their substantives, as in the Semitic languages, except when they form a compound; when they follow, there is an intervening *idhâfat*, as in modern Persian.

The sentence usually begins with the nominative, whose place may be taken by a pronoun which is often affixed to a particle (see pag. 93—94); then follows the object in the accusative; and the verb generally stands last and concludes the sentence. This position of the words is the same as in modern Persian; but it is not quite the same in old-Persian and Zand, where the verb frequently occupies the first place [1]) in the

1) This is occasionally the case also in the Pahlavî translations of the Zand-avesta, but then it is only a slavish imitation of the position of the words in Zand.

sentence, though it is also often found at the end. The construction in the Semitic languages is somewhat different; here the object generally follows the verb; but in the Assyrian inscriptions, it happens, not unfrequently, that the verb stands last, without any special reason (see the inscr. in Oppert, Expéd. en Mésop. II. pag. 295—296; comp. pag. 312, lin. 40—42. 47. 50. etc.).

Notwithstanding the prevalence of the Aryan character, in the construction of the sentences, there are also undeniable traces of a Semitic construction to be found. It is well known that the relative pronoun, in the Semitic languages, serves merely to express the relation of sentences to one another, and looks more like a particle than a relative pronoun, as used in the Aryan languages; if the sense requires the relative to be governed by a preposition, as in oblique cases, the preposition is not prefixed to the relative, but is quite separate from it, often after the verb, and always with a pronominal suffix referring to the principal word in the preceding sentence; for instance, Deut. 1, 22. Heb. הֶעָרִים אֲשֶׁר נָבוֹא אֲלֵיהֶן, Chald. קִרְוַיָּא דְּנֵיעוֹל לְהֵין 'the towns to which we shall come', literally 'the towns which we shall come to them'. Now there is the same construction in Pahlavî; for instance, Bund. 19, 16—17. [illegible] 'from which the seeds of all sorts of trees have grown', literally 'which the seeds of all sorts of trees from it have grown'; comp. also Bund. 19, 6. 22, 8—11. 24, 3. 26, 14. 28, 10. etc.

h) Conclusions on the character of Pahlavî, with special reference to that of other mixed languages.

From the foregoing short sketch of the principal grammatical features of Pahlavî, any reader, who does not adhere to preconceived opinions, will perceive that the Semitic element far outweighs the Iranian; so that its Iranian character becomes more than merely doubtful. We have seen that all the case signs and even the plural suffixes in the nouns; all the personal, demonstrative, interrogative and relative pronouns; all the numerals from one to ten; the most common verbs (including the auxiliaries) such as 'to be, to go, to come, to wish, to eat, to sleep, to write', etc.; almost all the prepositions, adverbs and conjunctions, and several important terminations for the formation of nouns, as well as a large majority of the words in general (at all events in the Sasanian inscriptions), are of Semitic origin. The only arguments that can be adduced in favor of an Iranian origin, are the verbal terminations, the suffixed pronouns and the construction of the sentences. The first two of these arguments vanish altogether, when we trace back the language sufficiently far, since I have shown from the Hâjiâbâd inscription, that in this early record of the Sasanian Pahlavî, the Iranian verbal terminations are completely wanting, and were only gradually added in the later inscriptions (see pag. 109), while the suffixed pronouns were originally Semitic (see pag. 93—94). Even in the construction of the sentences there are some Semitic traces; and the reason why it is generally of an Iranian character, will be presently explained. The defenders of the Iranian origin, who have hitherto been unacquainted with the language of the inscriptions (excepting a few words), will, no doubt, further point out, in favor of their views, that the Semitic nouns, verbs, and particles are often replaced by their Iranian equivalents, in the books. Now this fact, as well as all others which can be adduced in favor of the Iranian origin, is easily explained from Ibn Muqaffa's statement (pag. 38) and from the fact that the Parsis, down to the present day, never read the Semitic words which are written, but always pronounce their Iranian equivalents. To enable the Persians to read books in this strange way, which is an incontestable fact, a *farhang*, or glossary, containing the Semitic words alongside their Persian equivalents, was necessary, just like the one published in this volume; and that such a *farhang* existed in the Sasanian times, we learn from Ibn Muqaffa's statement.

The question now arises, can this strange fact (that Semitic words were written, but Iranian ones pronounced) be explained in any reasonable way by analogy? This can be answered in the affimative. The decipherment of the Assyrian inscriptions has shown, beyond doubt, that the very same fact existed in connection with the Assyrian. For instance, they wrote *atuya*, 'my father', but read *abuya* (Bis. lin. 1); they wrote *ud-shi*, *ud-um*, *ud-mu* and *ud-mi*, but read respectively *shamshi*, 'the sun', *yum*, 'day', *yummu* (nom. sing.) and *yummi* (pl. of *yum*) (see Norris, Assyr. Dict. I. pag. 210—211); they wrote *mat-ud* [1]) and *mat-ti*, but read *akshud*, 'I take, I hold', and *kishidti*, 'holding, capturing' (Oppert, Expéd. en Més. II. pag. 98). Here one sees, at the first glance, that the Assyrians added to the foreign word which they wrote, only the final syllable of the word which they pronounced. If the character, whose phonetic value was *ud*, meant 'sun', the Assyrians pronounced it *shamshu*, or *shamshi*, which was their name for 'the sun', comp. Heb. שֶׁמֶשׁ, and to prevent the character from being read in any other way, the syllabic sign for *shu*, or *shi*, was added to it; again, if the same character meant 'day', it was pronounced *yum*, *yummu*, or *yummi*, Heb. יוֹם, and to distinguish these different forms, the signs for the syllables *um*, *mu* and *mi* were respectively added to the original character.

If we ask for an explanation of this strange fact, the celebrated bilingual tablets of Sardanapal, which are now in the British Museum, give us a decisive answer. From them we learn, that the Assyrians must have received their system of writing, from a nation whose language was quite different from theirs; and they used the characters, which were partly ideographic and partly syllabic, for the same values as they had with the people who invented them. In this foreign tongue, which belonged to the Turanian stock, *adda* is 'father' (comp. Turkish اتا); now if the Assyrians wished to write 'father', they used the first character *ad*, or *at*, of *adda*, but pronounced it *ab* which was their own word for 'father'; and to express 'my father', they wrote *atuya*, but read it *abuya*; *u* being the Assyrian nominative termination, and *ya* the suffix meaning 'my', which, in the writing, were added to the foreign word *at* (see Oppert, Expéd. en Més. II. pag. 77—83. 98—100). This proceeding has its exact counterpart in the Pahlavî written words 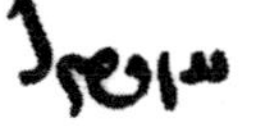 *abîtar*, 'father', and 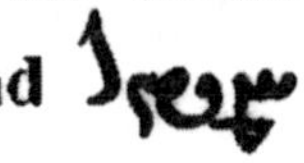

1) I use here the most common phonetic value attached to the sign which is pronounced *mat*, *kur*, *sat*, etc, and is the ideograph for 'country'.

amîtar, 'mother', being pronounced *patar* and *matar* respectively, and this Iranian pronunciation being indicated by the syllable *tar* added to the Semitic word.

Another very striking analogy is offered by Japanese writings, which are much intermixed with Chinese, and especially by the way in which the Japanese read Chinese texts. Japanese may be written entirely in Chinese characters which are then, however, not read in Chinese words, but in their Japanese equivalents; or secondly, the Chinese characters may be accompanied by a complete interlinear translation in the Japanese character; or thirdly, the Chinese characters may have merely the Japanese terminations added to them, with numerals for indicating the different position of the words in Japanese. This mode of reading the Chinese characters as if they were Japanese words, is called *yomi*, or *wa-kun*, which corresponds to the term Huzvâresh (see pag. 38. 43). [1] For the sake of illustration, I quote the beginning of the *Lun-yu*, the Confucian analecta, in Chinese, with the Japanese translation, or reading; the Chinese being expressed by capital letters: [2] Chin. TSE YUE: HIO URL SHI SI CHI PU YI YUE HU? 'the master said: is it not pleasant to study and daily practise it'? These words are read by the Japanese as follows: *si-no notamavaku*: *manande tokini korewo naravu mata yorokobasi-kara zu ya?* i. e. the master's saying (is): does it not again give pleasure to study and daily practise it? They do not merely pronounce the Japanese equivalent for each Chinese word, but they also add their grammatical particles and invert the construction. *Si-no* stands for TSE 'master', *no* being the genitive particle; *notamavaku*, 'saying', stands for YUE 'to speak'; *manande*, 'learning, studying', a gerund formed by the termination *de*, stands for HIO 'to learn'; URL 'and', is not expressed by a separate word, but by the preceding gerundial form, and the whole sentence

---

1) See Hoffmann, Japansche Spraakleer, pag. 29—35; Donker Curtius, Proeve eener Japansche Spraakkunst, pag 27—32; Léon de Rosny, Introduction à l'étude de la langue Japonaise, pag. 61—64.

2) The instance is taken from the work of Donker Curtius, pag. 30—31; but the analysis of the text is my own.

thus is contracted into 'by studying, practise it'; *tokini* = *toki*, 'day, time', + *ni*, dative particle, stands for SHI 'day'; *naravu*, 'to study', stands for SI 'to practise'; *korewo* = *kore*, 'this' + *wo*, accusative particle, stands for CHI 'this'; *zu* stands for PU 'not'; *mata*, 'another time', stands for YI 'also, even'; *yorokobasikara* = *yorokobasi*, 'giving pleasure', + *kara*, ablative particle, stands for YUE 'to be pleasant, to be pleased'; and *ya* stands for HU, an interrogative particle.

The second mode of adding to the Chinese a complete interlinear Japanese version, is analogous to the practice of writing a complete Pâzand version, word for word, under the Pahlavî, as is often done. While the third mode of merely adding the Japanese terminations and transposing numerals to the Chinese characters, is quite analogous to the way of writing the Huzvâresh words in the MSS. with Pazand terminations; as may be seen from the following imitation of the third mode of writing the sentence already quoted, with the Japanese complements: TSE*no* YUE: HIO*te*(*de*) URL SHI*ni* 2SI*vu* 1CHI*wo* 2PU*zu* YI 1YUE*kara* HU*ya*.

On comparing this text with the complete Japanese interlinear version, the reader will observe that the position of certain words, such as *kore* and *zu*, is here changed, but their proper order for pronunciation is indicated by numerals. This change is caused by the difference of construction in Chinese and Japanese; thus in Chinese, CHI 'it, this', must follow the verb, while in Japanese, the corresponding word *kore* with the particle *wo* must precede it; in like manner, the Chinese negative PU always precedes the verb, but the Japanese *zu* must follow the word to be negatived.

These analogous cases, together with Ibn Muqaffa's statement, and the mode of reading Pahlavî at the present day, clear up all the mystery attached to Pahlavî writings. Pahlavî, as written and read in the Huzvâresh mode, represents, in fact, two languages, one an Aramaic dialect, and the other a degenerated form of old Persian. The Aramaic text could be written in three ways, just as the Japanese when written with Chinese characters: *a)* Semitic words without any indication of their being read as if they were Iranian; of which class, the Sasanian version of the Hâjîâbâd inscription is an instance; *b)* Semitic words with the addition of Iranian pronominal suffixes and verbal terminations, and the occasional replacement of the Semitic words by their Iranian equivalents; which is the mode in which Pahlavî MSS. are written; *c)* Huzvâresh texts of the *b* class, with a complete interlinear version in the Zand character and Persian language, which is the so-called Pâzand.

Pahlavî is, therefore strictly speaking, no strangely mixed language, as it appears to be; but is either a purely Semitic language, with some admixture of Iranian words and a prevailing Iranian construction, or it is a purely Iranian tongue; the former is the case, if we look only to the way in which it is written, and the latter if we consider only the way in which it is read. We know now, that words like [illegible] *yehevûnt*, [illegible] *yehabûnêt*, [illegible] *yetîbûnastan*, etc., never really existed, but they were only written as symbols for بود 'he was', دهد 'he gives', نشستن 'to sit', etc.; their proper reading being indicated by the finals *t, êt, astan*, etc., which represented the terminations of the Iranian words that were to be read. But *yehevûn*, *yehabûn*, *yetîbûn*, etc., without the Iranian terminations, are by no means mere symbols, although the Persians may have used them as such; for they are true Semitic words, and must have been taken originally from some living language. The Iranian element prevails in the construction, for the simple reason that Iranian words were read; for instance, *malkân malkâ*, 'king of kings', was read *shâhanshâh* [1]), and therefore was not written according to the Semitic idiom, *malkâ malkân*.

---

1) Comp. Ammianus Marcellinus XIX. 2, 11: 'Persis Saporem et Saansaan adpellantibus et Pyrosen, quod rex regibus imperans et bellornm victor interpretatur'. The Persian king here mentioned was Sapor III, A. D. 308—381 and the war alluded to, was that with the Roman emperor Constantius, who returned to the western provinces of his empire about A. D. 350. The foregoing notice of Ammianus, that the Persians called Sapor III. by the title *saansaan*, i. e. *shâhanshâh*, 'king of kings', and not *malkân malkâ*, as the title is always written on his coins, clearly proves that *malkân malkâ* was pronounced *shâhanshâh*, as if it were a Persian word, and not according to its orthography and derivation as a Semitic one. This is a proof that the peculiar way of reading Pahlavî, as described by Ibn Muqaffa, existed as early as the middle of the 4th century A. D.

In order to show that, even if we had not the foregoing simple explanation of the origin of the strangely compounded words, Pahlavî could not be regarded as an Iranian language with an intermixture of Semitic words, as has been hitherto the general opinion, I adduce two further analogies from mixed languages, viz. Turkish and Singhalese.

The Turkish language consists of three elements, Turkish proper, Persian and Arabic. The number of Persian and Arabic words, especially in poetry, is overwhelming, and in excess of those of Turkish origin; but certain parts of speech, as well as the grammar and construction remain everywhere purely Turkish. The case terminations, pronouns and postpositions (used instead of prepositions) are all of Turkish origin, as are also the most common verbs, such as اولمق *olmaq*, 'to be', گلمك *gelmek*, 'to come, to arrive', ديمك *dimek*, 'to speak', وار *wâr*, 'it is', يوق *yoq*, 'it is not', etc., and many common nouns, such as اتا *ata*, 'father', اوغل *oghul*, 'son', يل *yel*, 'year', صو *sû*, 'water', قزل *qezel*, 'red', etc. The words taken from Persian and Arabic, are for the most part, abstract nouns, especially Arabic forms of the infinitive, used as a noun, and various participles; but they are never used to express the simplest ideas. For instance, they never use the Arabic term لَيْسَ, or the Persian نيست, to express the idea 'there is not', but they always use the phrase يوق در which is thoroughly Turkish; and they do not express the negative by the Arabic لا, or the Persian نه, but in the genuine Turkish way, by the affix *ma*, *me;* thus they do not say لا يازدم, or نه يازدم, for 'I have not written', but يازمدم *yazmadum* (from *yazmaq*, 'to write'). Now in Pahlavi, we find [illegible] [illegible] *lâ nepesht*, 'he did not write', [illegible] = לֵית 'there is not', etc.

More instructive is the analogy of the Singhalese, or Elu. This consists of two elements, the Sanscrito-Pâli and the proper Singhalese. [1]).

---

1) The Singhalese grammarians distinguish three kinds of words: *a) nipan*, original Singhalese, such as *rekur*, 'to make' (instead of *karanavâ*); *b) tasama*, Sanscrit and Pâli words with Elu terminations; *c) tabava*, words derived from Sanscrit and Pâli, with some slight alteration. See the Sidath Sangarawa translated by J. de Alwis, pag. 4.

The intermixture of the foreign (Sanscritic) element, is here much more extensive than in any other known language. Not only all the numerals, but even some of the most common verbs, such as *yanavâ*, 'to go', and *karanavâ*, 'to make', are taken from Pâli, and also in conjugating the verbs, besides the genuine Singhalese mode, which is very imperfect, they use that of the Pâli (with the terminations *mi, hi, ê*, etc.) which is more complete. But the auxiliary verb, *innavâ*, is Elu, and so are also the pronouns [1]) and case signs; for instance, *api*, 'we'; *umbâ*, 'thou'; *umbạlâ*, 'you'; *mê*, 'this'; the postposition *gê* of the genitive case, *ṭa* of the dative, *gen* of the ablative, etc.; none of which can be explained from Sanscrit, or Pâli.

The intermixture of a foreign element cannot certainly go further than it has in Elu. But if the Semitic element in Pahlavi were the foreign one, we should have a language in which the pronouns and case signs were all foreign, for we have seen they are all Semitic. Now as no language exists, whose pronouns and case signs are all foreign, we are justified in regarding the Semitic element as not being the foreign one in Pahlavi, which we can, therefore, no longer consider an Iranian language.

Having now shown the impossibility of classing the so-called Huzvâresh with the Iranian languages, and having explained the strange-sounding forms and words of that language, in a reasonable way, I have to add merely a short remark, on the complete disappearance of the Semitic words of the Pahlavi, from modern Persian. As we have seen, the Persians, when reading Huzvâresh texts, substituted for each Semitic word its Iranian equivalent; in the course of time, they began to make this substitution also when writing; and as soon as they began to write the texts just as they pronounced them, that is, when they wrote only Persian words, their writings became modern Persian. This is the simplest way of explaining the total disappearence of all the Âramaic words of Pahlavi,

1) The pronouns *mama*, 'I', and *to*, 'thou', may be explained from Sanscrit; but their plurals *api*, 'we', and *topi*, 'you', will baffle all attempts at such a derivation. See F. Müller, in the 'linguistic part' of the 'Reise der Novara', pag. 209.

from modern Persian; which certainly would not have occurred if the Aramaic words had formed part of the spoken language. Some slight Aramaic traces, however, still remain in the grammar, as the *idhâfat* and some terminations, such as the pl. suffix *ân*, clearly show.

5. On the origin and age of Pahlavî.

As I have already treated of this question, in the introduction to the Zand-Pahlavî glossary, I shall confine myself here to briefly summing up the principal results I have arrived at, and adding such observations and remarks on the subject, as have been suggested to me by a continuous study of it.

It has hitherto been the general belief, as the reader will have seen from my sketch of Pahlavî studies (pag. 1—32), that Pahlavî was a language which originated, in a mixture of Semitic and Iranian elements, on the frontiers of Iran and Chaldæa (Savad), in the first, or second, century A. D., and thence spread gradually over the whole Persian empire, under the rule of the Sasanian dynasty, even to the confines of India. But against such an opinion, several strong arguments can be urged.

Firstly, it would be surprising, if a curious jargon of Semitic and Iranian words and inflections (in which the former element even outweighs the latter), such as Pahlavî appears to superficial observers, had been adopted by the Sasanian kings (A. D. 226—640) as their official language, into which the sacred books were translated, and in which an extensive literature, sacred and profane, arose. And this adoption of a newly-formed jargon, for such purposes, would be still more surprising, if we reflected that the Sasanian kings were very zealous promoters of Persian ascendancy, and restorers of the Zoroastrian religion. We may search the history of nations and languages in vain for a similar instance. It has never happened that a mere jargon, originating on a frontier (from the intercourse of the inhabitants speaking different languages) has become the official and ecclesiastical language of a large empire for four centuries. The reasons for adopting a foreign language, or for giving preponderance to a foreign element, are generally of a political, or a religious, nature. Thus, wherever Arabic has spread and gained an influence over any native tongue, such as Persian, Turkish and Malay, it has been owing to the spread of the Mohamedan religion, the sacred writings of which are in Arabic. Similarly, the influence of Sanscrit and Pâli over foreign tongues, such as Singhalese and Barmese, can be accounted for, only by the spread of Buddhism, the sacred books of which were composed both in Pâli and Sanscrit. Chinese writing and literature extended over Korea, Japan and Cochin China, in consequence of early conquests by the Chinese. Latin became the official and ecclesiastical language of Europe, in the middle ages, in consequence of the early Roman conquests, and the establishment of the Romish church over all the Christian nations of the west. Hindûstânî, which is a mixture of Sanscritic, Persian and Arabic elements, did not arise before the Mohamedan conquest of India. The Anglo-Saxon of Britain was not mingled with French till after the Norman conquest. Even Greek, which was the language most widely spread at the beginning of the Christian era, owed its great diffusion to conquest, for although the Hellenic nation was rather a colonizing than a conquering race, yet colonists are always conquerors more or less; and the spread of their language in the east, was chiefly owing to the Macedonian conquests, and the establishment of the Seleucidan and Bactrian empires with Greek rulers.

Now none of the reasons which led to the diffusion of any of the above-mentioned languages in a foreign country, or to their production of mixed languages, can be shown to have caused the formation of Pahlavî, if we assign its origin to the first, or second, century of the Christian era. No Semitic nation conquered Persia at that time; nor did any religion, whose sacred language was an Aramaic dialect, spread over the whole Persian empire at that period, and upset that of Zoroaster; nor yet did any foreign literature exercise such a paramount influence over Persia, at that time, as to give birth to a new language of a mixed character, by the blending of its words and phrases with the Persian tongue. Though Greek literature was then most widely spread, and was not unknown in

Persia, it left but very few traces in the Persian language. The Christian literature of the Syrian church, then in its infancy, seems to have exercised no influence over the indigenous literature, as we find no specifically Christian terms in Pahlavî books. Although Christianity began to spread in Persia, under the Sasanian rule, and gave birth to a new branch of religious literature, now wholly lost, it gained no influence over Zoroastrianism, which was very hostile to the new religion, for at the instigation of the Magi, the Christians were persecuted by the kings and put to death. If even so polished and refined a literature as the Greek, left so few traces in the Persian language, far less change can be attributed to the influence of the exclusively religious literature of a sect, which was barely tolerated and sometimes persecuted. To assume otherwise, would be equivalent to asserting, that the colloquial jargon of the modern Jews had exercised some influence over the languages of the European nations, among whom they are scattered, which would be simply absurd. Thus we see that history furnishes not a single valid reason for the origin of Pahlavî, as a mixed language, in the first and second centuries; but it rather supplies arguments against such an origin.

Secondly, the complete disappearance of the Aramaic words of Pahlavî, in its successor, the modern Persian, even as early as the time of Firdûsî (A. D. 1000), could not be explained, if Pahlavî had been a frontier language, or jargon, of Semitic and Iranian elements. When foreign words have once become naturalized, and been employed in standard works of literature, they will, for the most part, never disappear, but will henceforth remain a part of the language; such has been the case with the Persian and Arabic words in the Indian vernaculars, with the Latin words in the Teutonic languages, and with the Arabic ones in modern Persian. If the Aramaic words had formed a part of the Persian language, as spoken during the Sasanian times, there must still have been some relics of them, in so early a poem as that of Firdûsî; but not a trace of them can be found; even the royal title *malkân malkâ*, had disappeared. But this disappearance is easily accounted for, when one understands the real character of the Pahlavî writings, as set forth above (pag. 121.) It was only in a few grammatical points, that traces of a Semitic element remained; but these are easily accounted for, if one considers that, in the constant practice of reading Semitic words as if they were Persian, some minute details (such as the plural termination, the *idhâfat*, the conjunction ↄ and some terminations) which were not changed when reading Semitic texts in Persian, would naturally be preserved, when the texts began to be written as they were pronounced.

Thirdly, the whole character of Pahlavî, as described in the fourth section, is opposed to the supposition that it was a frontier language of the first, or second, century. At that time, and indeed for many previous centuries, various Semitic alphabets existed, which comprised only a limited number of letters with a specific phonetic value attached to each; it would therefore have been very strange, if the Sasanian kings had chosen for official use, so clumsy a kind of writing as the Pahlavî, in which the various groups of letters were regarded merely as symbols for Persian words. There was certainly no reason for their publishing documents, and inscriptions on their coins, in Semitic words, if they were always to be read in Persian. And if the Semitic words were used for the benefit of their subjects of Semitic origin, then the language ought to have been of Semitic construction, so as to have been readily understood by the Semites. But Pahlavî, even in Sasanian times, was not well adapted for either Persians, or Semites; the Persians could not read it, till they had learned the Persian meaning of some five hundred symbols, which must have been too unpleasant a task for a ruling race to set themselves; while the Semites must have found the symbols scarcely intelligible, although they were really Semitic words, as they did not clearly represent any Semitic language. The verbs were used only in the plural form, as we have seen, and the persons were expressed by suffixes joined to particles. Now we possess Aramaic texts of the first and second centuries A. D. (in Chaldee and Syriac), and the persons, in them, are not expressed in such a manner, but by prefixes and affixes to the verb itself, as in all the old Semitic languages. It is evident from my remarks in section 4 (*i* and *h*), that the Semitic language which underlies the Pahlavî, was not left unchanged, but was adapted to the Persian mind; and the Semitic texts were written with a view to their being read by the Persians as if they were Persian. But as this mode of writing and reading had no convenience to recommend it, we must suppose that the Sasanian kings would not have adopted it, unless they had found it already existing as a time-honored practice.

Fourthly, the fact that two Pahlavî dialects, similar in character, were used in the earlier Sasanian inscriptions, precludes the supposition that Pahlavî was a frontier language of the first and second centuries. For if this view were correct, we should have to admit the existence of two jargons, which both originated on the frontiers of Persia, Assyria and Babylonia, and both spread over the Persian empire, at about the same time. But can such an opinion bear a critical examination for a moment? It may be answered that one jargon, the so-called Chaldæo-Pahlavi, might have been in use one or two centuries earlier, under the Arsacidan rule; while the other jargon, the Sasanian Pahlavî, might have come into use in the time of Ardeshîr Bâbegân, and superseded the former. But it would be very strange if each dynasty, the Arsacidan as well as the Sasanian, had adopted as its official language, a separate jargon, originating on a frontier merely through the intercourse of two neighbouring nations; both jargons, though distinct, being formed on the same principles. Why did they not rather adopt the Persian language, which has always been the vernacular of Persia, since that country became known in history?

Having shown the great improbability, if not impossibility, of the supposition that Pahlavî was a frontier language, which originated only a short time before Ardeshîr Bâbegân ascended the throne of Iran, it is now incumbent on me to offer a more satisfactory explanation of its age and origin.

The first question to be considered, is whether there are any inscriptions, or literary compositions, in either the Sasanian, or Chaldæo-Pahlavî, anterior to the third century of the Christian era? This can be answered in the affirmative; as the reader will find, on reference to pag. 30, that there are legends extant, on coins from the south of Persia, in the so-called Chaldæo-Pahlavi character and language, and Dr. Levy has shown that these cannot be later than the third, or beginning of the fourth, century B. C.; they clearly exhibit the words מלכא *malkâ*, 'king', and זי אלה *zi alah*, 'of God', *zî* being the relative pronoun in Pahlavî (see pag. 74), but used to express the genitive.

The legends on the so-called Abd-Zohar coins [1]) present us with an earlier form of Pahlavî; for they belong to the so-called Satrap coins and, for numismatical reasons, cannot be later than the latter part of the Achæmenian rule, which was overthrown by Alexander B. C. 330; and they may even go back to the fifth century B. C. As they are important for proving the antiquity of Pahlavî, I shall make some remarks upon their language. The legend, which can be restored with some degree of certainty, by comparing different specimens of the same coin, is in a very early form of Aramaic character, and runs as follows: מזדי זי על עבד זהראו חלך. If this be written in Pahlavi characters, no alteration in the words, or their position, is necessary to render it into pure Sasanian Pahlavî, thus [Pahlavi script] = [Pahlavi script] *mizdî zi ûl Abd Zoharâû Khalk*. Now *mizdî* is an Iranian word which is used in Pahlavi (see the index, pag. 156, s. v. *mazd*) and means 'reward, wages'; *î* being the final vowel which is, as we have seen, so frequently found at the end of nouns, in the Sasanian inscriptions, e. g. *bagî* for *bag*, *chîtâkî* for *chîtâk*, *Shahpûhrî* for *Shahpûhr*, etc. (regarding its origin, see pag. 88—90); *zî* is the relative pronoun used throughout the Pahlavî (see index, pag. 241—242, s. v. *zêsh*, *zîam*); *ûl* [Pahlavi script] = [Pahlavi script] (trad. *var*) is identical with the preposition על (initial ע being sometimes expressed by the Pahlavî [Pahlavi script], see index, pag. 222. 231) and is used everywhere, in Pahlavî, as a sign of the dative, in the sense

1) See Duc de Luynes, Essai sur la numismatique des Satrapies sous les rois Achæménides, pag. 26—30; Supplement à l'Essai, planche III et IV; Blau, De numis Achæmenidarum, pag. 5. 11. 12; Levy, Beiträge zur aramäischen Münzkunde Kleinasiens, in the Zeitschrift der Deutschen Morgenländischen Gesellschaft, vol. XV. pag. 623 et seq.

of 'to, for'. That על was used occasionally in this sense, in the Aramaic dialects, we know not only from books, but also from inscriptions; thus we read in Dan. 4, 24: מִלְכִּי יִשְׁפַּר עֲלָיךְ 'let my counsel be acceptable unto thee'; Ezra 7, 18: מָה דִי עֲלָיךְ וְעַל־אֶחָיךְ יֵיטַב 'whatsoever shall seem good to thee and to thy brethren'; comp. also Dan. 6, 19 and Ezra 5, 17. In the oldest inscription known to exist at Palmyra, No. 30 [1]), which is dated 304 of the Seleucidan era = B. C. 9, על is also used as a sign of the dative, like לְ, thus: קברא ...... די בנו עלוהי בנוהי 'the tomb ..... which his sons built for him'; comp. the frequent formula על חיוהי 'for his welfare', in that large class of Palmyrenian inscriptions, termed 'inscriptions religieuses', by Count de Vogüé (see pag. 55—74 of his work); על is also found with the same meaning in the inscriptions of Hauran, thus, 2, c. (de Vogüé, pag. 93): די הו בנה על בעשמין 'which he made to the Lord of Heaven'. Returning to the legend on the coins; Abd-Zoharâû was the name of the satrap of Cilicia, under whose rule the coins were struck; here the final *û*, which is a characteristic of the book Pahlavî, is remarkable, as it is frequently found at the end of proper names, on the coins of other satraps of the same period, comp. פרנבזו *Pharnabazû*, תבלו *Tabalû*, etc. (see Zand-Pahl. Gl. pag. XXIV). Although this final *û*, in names, is not found in Chaldee and Syriac books, we meet with it in the Aramaic inscriptions of Palmyra and Hauran, and those of the Nabathæan kings; thus, Palm. 4, 2. מקימו (in the Greek translation) *Μοκιμου* [2]), 15, 1. מלכו *Μαλχου*, 18, 2. עזיזו *Αζιζου*, 11, 1. שריכו *Soraïkû*, 30, 2. כהילו *Kohîlû*; Haur. 3, 2. מעירו *Μοαιερου*, 3, 4. כדו *Kaddû*, כלבו *Kalabû* (de Vogüé, pag. 99); Nabath. 3, 2. 3. אושו *Ausû*, 6. רוחו *Rûahû*, מתבו *Matabû*, אכלבו *Akalbû*, נבטו *Nabṭû*, etc. It is also found in ancient names in the Old Testament, comp. יִתְרוֹ *Yithrô* (Jethro), מְתוּשָׁאֵל *M'tû-shael*

---

1) In Count M. de Vogüé's Inscriptions Sémitiques, text, pag. 37.

2) The *ου* in the Greek translations represents the genitive case, as the names generally follow the words בר 'son', or צלמא די 'image of'; but the ו in the Aramaic names, is no genitive termination, as it occurs also where the name is in the nominative case.

(Methusael), שמואל *Sh'mûel* (Samuel), etc. The last word of the legend, חלך *Khalk*, is the name of Cilicia in Asia Minor, which was governed by native rulers who were dependent upon Persia; it is enumerated in the list of subject provinces, in the cuneiform inscription of Naksh-i Rustam, under the form *Karaka*, which cannot mean 'Carthage', as has been supposed.

The meaning of the whole legend on the Abd-Zohar coins, is clearly as follows: 'pay (i. e. soldier's pay) which (belongs) to Abd-Zohar of Cilicia', i. e. which is to be distributed by him to his soldiers. The language of this legend, as we have seen, contains four characteristic features of the Pahlavî of Sasanian times: *a)* the final *î* in *mizdî*; *b)* the relative pronoun זי *zî*; *c)* על in the sense of a dative characteristic, or the preposition 'to, for'; *d)* the final *û* in *Abd-Zoharû*. Those who may object to my opinion that the language of this legend is identical with the primitive Sasanian Pahlavî, will probably say, that it represents only that Aramaic language which was current in Cilicia, during the Achæmenian rule, and does not furnish any argument for the higher age of Pahlavî. But among the four characteristics already mentioned, at least two are specifically characteristic of that Aramaic dialect which underlies the Sasanian Pahlavî; these are, first, the relative זי *zî*, which is די *dî* in all other Aramaic dialects, such as Chaldee, Syriac, Palmyrene, Hauranitic, Nabathæan, etc.; second, the final *î* in מזדי *mizdî*, which is wanting in the other dialects.

After a fair consideration of the arguments here adduced, which have been based on the careful numismatic researches of De Luynes, Blau, Levy, etc., and on my own investigations, it will be hardly possible to deny that the Semitic dialect of the Pahlavî was in use, in the Persian empire, as early as the fourth century B. C.; at any rate, *before* the Macedonian conquest. The question then arises, did it originate during the later period of the Achæmenian rule, or at a much earlier time? As the Achæmenian rulers were of Persian origin, and employed three languages simultaneously, in their cuneiform inscriptions, viz. Persian, Susian and Assyrian, we cannot see any reason for their giving a preference to a Semitic dialect in the provinces subject to them, unless they found it already existing and firmly established; especially as this Semitic dialect of the Pahlavî was not identical with the Assyrian, as exhibited in the Assyrian versions of the Persian cuneiform inscriptions; which versions represent, on the whole, the same language as the records of Niniveh and Babylon, and this seems to have been the ancient Assyrian as employed on monuments and in literary records, but differing from the language commonly used by the people. The latter, which was a true Aramaic dialect, was written, even at an early period, in the so-called Phenician character, of which the Pahlavî alphabets are descendants.

These characters are found on the Assyrian weights which go back to the eighth century B. C., and also on clay tablets (now in the British Museum) which must have been inscribed, at any rate, before the destruction of Niniveh, B. C. 606. As two characteristic features of Pahlavî are easily discovered, in one of the latter inscriptions[1]), I give it in full, with the necessary remarks, as follows: בחצרן V לם סרנרג שערן זי בר מלכא על נבירבן מן עירן V ב VII. Sir H. Rawlinson explains it as an order for the assignment of grain, and I think his opinion is, on the whole, well founded, though I differ from him in some particulars. The first five words evidently contain the date, given in the usual Assyrian manner, by naming the year after the eponym; ב is the Hebrew preposition בְּ which is used, with regard to time, in the sense of 'about, at', e. g. בַּיּוֹם 'at this day', i. e. 'now', כָּעֵת 'at this time'; חצרן is the Syrian month ܚܙܝܪܢ; לם is 'eponymy', and סרנרג the name of the eponym, which is, however, not to be found in the lists hitherto known, which extend from B. C. 938 to 642[2]); hence we may conclude that the date of this inscription is pro-

1) A facsimile of it, with a transliteration in Hebrew characters, is given by Sir H. Rawlinson in the 'Cuneiform inscriptions of Western Asia', vol. II. pag. 70, No. 16; and with a commentary, in the Journal of the Royal Asiatic Society, new series, vol. I. pag. 223 - 227.

2) See Oppert, in Zeitschr. der Deut. Morg. Ges. vol. XXIII. pag. 138—144; and Sir H. Rawlinson, Cuneiform inscriptions of Western Asia. vol. II. pag. 68—69.

bably between B. C. 641 and 606, the latter being the date of the end of the Assyrian rule. שערן is the Chald. שְׂעָרִין, שְׂעוֹרִין, Heb. שְׂעֹרִים 'grains of barley', which is generally used in the plural. זי is the relative pronoun and one of the characteristic features of the Semitic dialect of the Pahlavi; it is also found in other inscriptions of the seventh century B. C., as in No. 2 of the bilingual readings by Sir H. Rawlinson, and in No. V [1]) of the appendix to them. בר מלכא 'the son of the king', i. e. 'prince' corresponds to the Pahlavi [illegible]. על is here used in the sense of a dative characteristic, just as on the Abd-Zohar coins (see pag. 133) and in Pahlavi. נבירבן looks like the name of him to whom the grain is assigned, and is probably a plural, signifying a title. מן עירן can hardly be the name of the weight, as Sir H. Rawlinson supposes, though it is followed by the numeral V; for מן must be the preposition מִן 'from, among', and not מנה (as the name of the weight is always written on the Assyrian lion-weights), since final vowels are not left unexpressed in the ancient Aramaic, as they are in Phenician; עירן is evidently a plural, and can be traced either to עִיר 'town', which is not, however, common in Chaldee, or to עִיר 'a guardian', used of guardian angels in Dan. 4, 10. 14, 20. ב with the numeral VII, is the symbol for the respective measure of grain which is assigned. I would propose to translate the whole inscription thus: 'On the 5th day of the month *Khaziran*, in the eponymy of *Sar-Narag* (i. e. in the year called after his name), barley grains of the royal prince (have been assigned) to Nabiraban, among the five guardians (of the place), to the amount of 7 *b*...' (the name of the measure is uncertain). It is thus clearly an assignment of grain to some high court officers, from the granary of a prince.

Before leaving this old inscription, I have to remark upon the probable pronunciation of the plural forms שערן and עירן; the final syllable may have been pronounced either *în*, or *ân*, but as the *î*, in *în*, is

1) See Journal of the Roy. As. Soc. new series. vol. I. pag. 232—234; comp. also Levy, 'Siegel und Gemmen mit aramäischen, etc. Inschriften' (Breslau 1869) pag. 6.

generally expressed in Chaldee, thus ין־ָ, while the *â*, in *ân*, is frequently unexpressed, thus ן־ָ, and as *î* is several times expressed in the inscription (and not omitted, as in Phenician), I think it most probable that we should read *seorân* and *'îrân*, which forms quite agree with the plurals in Pahlavî. It is also deserving of special notice, that the end of each word, except די, is indicated by a dot, unless it concludes a line, or is followed by numeral strokes. This mode of indicating the division of the words, in all cases which might admit of doubt, is the more remarkable, as it is not usual in Semitic inscriptions; in Phenician, Palmyrene, Nabathæan and other inscriptions, no dividing dot is used, and in most of them, such as the Phenician, no additional space even is left at the end of a word; it is only in the Himyaritic inscriptions, that the words are divided by a vertical stroke. Among early writings, this mode of marking the ends of the words, has its analogy in the old-Persian of the cuneiform inscriptions, where the words are divided by oblique strokes and in the Avesta, where the end of each word is indicated by a dot. May there not be some connection between this old Iranian practice, and the system adopted in the Assyrian inscription above-noticed? [1])

We have now traced the Semitic dialect of Pahlavî as far back as the seventh century B. C. According to our investigation, it is identical with that form of the Assyrian language which was written in the so-called Phenician character, and which was, no doubt, spoken at Niniveh, whence it spread, with the Assyrian rule, over all the subject provinces. After the Assyrian empire had been destroyed by the Medes and Babylonians, the Assyrian language continued to be used, for a long time, in

---

1) It appears from a letter from Jerusalem, dated 18th Jan. 1870 and published in the Moniteur of 5th Febr., that an inscription of more than thirty lines, in old Phenician characters, has lately been found, eastward of the Dead Sea, in which the words are separated by dots, and the phrases by vertical lintes. It is said to be commemorative of the deeds of Mesha, king of Moab, mentioned in 2 Kings 3. (about B. C. 900); and its language is stated to differ from Hebrew only in some orthographical peculiarities; what relationship it may bear to the Assyrian vernacular has yet to be determined.

the former dominions of the conquered state; thus alone can we explain its use, in the legends on the coins of Cilicia and other western provinces, in Achæmenian times.

Another strong proof of the high antiquity of the Semitic element of Pahlavî, is the peculiar way in which it is read, which can only be explained by the supposition of an original ideographic writing, such as is frequent enough in the Assyrian cuneiform inscriptions. We have seen that the Assyrians read the Turanian ideograms as if they represented Assyrian words, in the same way as the Japanese now read Chinese characters as though they stood for Japanese words. But as Pahlavî is written with phonetic, and not with ideographic, characters, it appears strange that the Iranians did not, from the first, use the Pahlavî alphabet to write the words in their own language, instead of writing Semitic words, and reading them as if they were Iranian. Those who do not believe in the high antiquity of Pahlavî, but prefer to cling to the idea of its much later origin, may explain this strange fact by asserting that the Semitic words were retained, either because the Pahlavî alphabet, being of Semitic origin, was better adapted for expressing Semitic words than Iranian ones, or because the higher classes of Iranians, especially the priests, preferred such a mode of writing, in order to conceal the contents of their books from laymen, or the lower classes in general. But neither of these explanations can be accepted. With regard to the first, it may be remarked that, though the Semitic characters were intended only to express such sounds as occur in Semitic idioms, the Iranians might have adapted them to the phonetic requirements of their own language, just as easily as the Greeks who adopted the Phenician alphabet, or the modern Persians and Indian Mohamedans when they took to the Arabic alphabet. The second explanation is contradicted by the fact, that the Sasanian kings employed Pahlavî in their public inscriptions and the legends on their coins; for it cannot be supposed that the kings would have chosen, for public purposes, a language and a writing which was understood by only a very small number of their subjects. In fact, no other explanation will suffice, but the supposition of an original ideographic writing. There can be no doubt that the learned, among the Iranians, were acquainted with the cuneiform writing of their Assyrian conquerors. As its study was difficult and troublesome, it is natural to suppose that they used, in order to facilitate their studies, transliterations into Aramaic (the so-called Phenician) characters [1]). As a cuneiform ideogram, representing an entire word, might be pronounced either as a Semitic, or as an Iranian word, at the option of the reader, the Iranians probably regarded the Semitic transliterations of the cuneiform signs, merely as equivalent ideograms, and accustomed themselves to read these, as well as the cuneiform ideograms, only as Iranian words. In the course of time, and chiefly on account of the introduction of other writing materials, such as prepared ox-hides, or sheep-skins, the cuneiform writing disappeared altogether from ordinary records, and was reserved for monumental purposes; but the transliterations in Aramaic characters remained, and continued to be pronounced as Iranian words, in the same manner as their cuneiform equivalents had formerly been.

The origin of Pahlavî, we have now seen, can be sought for only during the period of the Assyrian rule, which lasted, over Iran, for 520 years (Herodotus I. 95), and was established as early as the twelfth century B. C., if not earlier. In the whole history of Iran, from Assyrian down to Arsacidan times, there is no other period, during which its rise and spread could be explained in any reasonable way. It is not however to be supposed, that the Iranians adopted the Assyrian language in its purity. They learned it as a conquered race learns the language of their conquerors, and mingled it with words of their own vernacular idiom; but those parts of speech which are decisive of the character of a language, such as pronouns, prepositions, particles, the most common nouns

---

1) There are still some bi-lingual tablets extant, in Assyrian cuneiform writing, with a transliteration, or rather a translation, into Aramaic characters and the vulgar Assyrian dialect which underlies the Pahlavî. They have been published by Sir H. Rawlinson, with an explanation, in the Journal of the R. As. Soc., new series, vol. I. pag. 187—246.

and verbs, the declension and even some suffixes, remained Semitic. It was only in the conjugation of the verbs, and in the construction of the sentences, that Iranian influence gradually prevailed. This is not surprising, for the Assyrian way of denoting tenses and moods is much inferior to the Aryan; the Assyrians used only one principal tense, the so-called aorist (with the personal characteristics prefixed), and active and passive participles, whilst the Iranians used a present and three past tenses, besides various forms of participles, and different moods, such as the optative and conjunctive, which the Assyrians could not well distinguish. It was quite natural that the Iranians should prefer the passive construction with the past participle (see pag. 106. 109. 110.) as the most simple [1]), for it required hardly any proper knowledge of the Assyrian conjugation. The persons were expressed by pronominal suffixes, joined to Semitic particles which were generally placed at the beginning of the sentence. As we have seen above (pag. 106), some ready-made passive participles were taken from Assyrian; but along with them, the Iranians used the Assyrian aorist forms in the plural, frequently omitting the initial *y* (see pag. 105), but treated them as past participles. This is evident on comparing the Sasanian and Chaldæo-Pahlavî versions of the Hâjiâbâd inscription; for in the latter, there are regular Assyrian past participles fem. in *ît*, such as שדית, רמית and בנית; whereas in the former there are forms ending in *n* (*un*), such as [illegible] *shadîtun* = [illegible], and [illegible] *ramîtun* = [illegible]. The prevalence of the passive construction in Pahlavi, accounts for two remarkable circumstances; firstly, the almost total absence of the Semitic forms of the active participle, and secondly, the want of a proper passive voice. When the Iranians read the Semitic texts in the Persian language, they had to add the terminations of the present tense, the conjunctive mood, etc., as these could not be expressed by past participles.

1) A similar course is adopted by the modern *pandits* in India, when they write and speak Sanscrit. Only those who have made grammar a special study, employ the perfect and aorist tenses; but the larger number, who possess a mere smattering of grammar, always use the past participles with the instrumental case, to express any past event.

This Pahlavî form of Assyrian remained one of the recognized languages, long after the downfall of the Assyrian empire. We find it in the Persian provinces under the Achæmenian rule, and after the conquest of Persia by Alexander the Great, and the establishment of the Arsacidan empire (see pag. 30). Under the kings of the latter dynasty, we find only that dialect used which is now styled Chaldæo-Pahlavî, and which remained in official use, alongside the Sasanian Pahlavî, until the middle, or end, of the third century A. D. Of this dialect we have discovered no traces, anterior to the legends on the so-called sub-Parthian coins (see pag. 30), which are later than the Macedonian conquest, but may be older than the foundation of the Arsacidan dynasty, and may thus range between B. C. 320 and 260. These coins are chiefly found in the south-west of Persia, where this dialect seems to have prevailed; and as it bears, in some features, a striking resemblance to Chaldee (comp. the plural in *în*, instead of *ân*, and the use of אלהא for 'god', which is not found in the Sasanian Pahlavî), it may be taken as an offspring of the Babylonian which, no doubt, spread widely, in consequence of the conquests of Nebuchadnezzar, early in the sixth century B. C.; but it seems never to have spread eastwards, as the Sasanian Pahlavî did, which we have identified with the vulgar Assyrian.

The fact that Ardeshîr Bâbegân and his successors made the Assyrian-Pahlavî, and not the Chaldæan one, the official language of their whole empire, proves clearly that the former was much better known in Iran than the latter, especially in the central and eastern provinces. But I doubt if the greater extension of the Assyrian Pahlavî was the only reason why the Sasanian kings made it their state language, in preference to Persian. There must have been some literature, chiefly of a religious character, existing in that language, before the Sasanian dynasty was founded; and as Ardeshîr Bâbegân was the restorer of the Zoroastrian religion, it may be supposed that he would naturally give the preference to a language which had been, for centuries, the medium by which the Zoroastrian traditions had been preserved, and which had thus obtained the character of a certain degree of sacredness.

But those who hold that Pahlavî is a frontier language of the second century A. D., may object that no Pahlavî literature existed before the Sasanian times, and assert that all the Pahlavî works, we now possess, are of later date, and not anterior to the seventh and eighth centuries A. D. It is quite true, that no Pahlavî work is now extant, which is older than the third century A. D. 1), that is, later than the foundation of the Sasanian dynasty; but this does not prove that no literature existed, in the Assyrian Pahlavî, before the time of Ardeshîr Bâbegân. In fact, we have every reason to believe that comments upon the *Avesta*, or even verbatim translations of parts of it, existed in the Pahlavî language, long before the Sasanian times. According to the *Ardâi-Virâf-nâmeh* (which was probably composed some time in the reign of Shâpûr II., but certainly

1) The earliest which has reached us, seems to be the *Kâr-nâmeh* of Ardeshir Bâbegân, of which I possess a copy. This comprises 46 pages, each containing 11 or 12 lines, and each line about 6 or 7 words; it was carefully copied for me, by my friend Destur Hoshengji himself. This little work describes Ardeshîr's usurpation of the throne and his wars with Ardavân, the last king of the Arsacidan dynasty. Tradition ascribes its authorship to Ardeshîr himself (according to *Masûdî*, see Quatremère, Journal des Savants for 1840, pag. 350; comp. S. de Sacy, Mémoires sur diverses antiquités de la Perse, pag. 280); but this opinion is contradicted by the book itself, since it concludes with the accession of Hormazd I. to the throne of Iran (A. D. 269), and the acknowledgement of his rule by the *kîsâr-i Arûmâ,ân*, i. e. the Roman emperor, the ruler of Kâbûl and Hindûstân ([Pahlavi]), and the *khâkân* ([Pahlavi]) of the Turks ([Pahlavi]). In the postscript, a blessing is invoked upon the first three kings of the Sasanian dynasty, viz. *Artakhshadr Pâpakân* ([Pahlavi]), *Shahpûhr Artakhshadrân* ([Pahlavi]) and *Auharmazd Shahpûhrân* ([Pahlavi]). As the blessing is not extended to any of the following kings, we are entitled to assign the composition of this work, which has reached us only in a fragmentary state, to the reign of Hormazd I. (A. D. 269—271). If it had been composed during the reign of one of Hormazd's successors, the name of the reigning sovereign could not well have been omitted by the author, in the blessing he invokes upon the Sasanian kings.

not later than the sixth century), the people's ignorance of the religious books was so great that there was no Destur, nor any one, who knew the religion [1]). Though this statement may be exaggerated, we learn thus much from it, that the knowledge of the Avesta was certainly not in a flourishing state, among the priesthood, at that time. Even in the time of Ardeshîr Bâbegân, the priests do not seem to have been great proficients in the study of the sacred books; for the Dîn-kart states, that Herbad Tosre collected [2]), by order of this king, all the fragments of the Avesta which were scattered about the country; hence it follows that the priests must have been very careless about their sacred books, otherwise collections of them would have been already in existence. Now the language of the Avesta, which is commonly called Zand (though very improperly, as we shall presently see), possesses a large number of inflections, and its grammar, as far as we know, was never studied and propagated as a distinct science, as has been done with that of Sanscrit in India; on the other hand, the Persian language of Ardeshîr's time, had lost the majority of its ancient inflections; how can it be supposed, therefore, that priests could be found, in his time, who could muster such a knowledge of Zand and its numerous inflections, as the Pahlavî translators of the Vendidad evidently possessed? There is no probability that any such existed, and that is the opinion of all Parsi priests of the present day. We may further add, that if any of the Sasanian kings had

---

1) See Zand-Pahl. Gl. pag. XLI. This sad state of things was altered in the time of *Adarbâd Mahraspand*, who is expressly mentioned in the *Ardâi-Virâf-nâmeh*, but as unfortunately no royal name of the Sasanian dynasty occurs, we cannot exactly state the time. In the Dîn-kart (vol. I. pag. 5 of my MS.), an *Adarbâd* ([illegible]) is mentioned, as a restorer of the Nosks of the Avesta, who lived during the reign of Shâpûr II.; but as the name of his father is not added, we cannot be quite sure of his identity with the great *Adarbâd Mahraspand*. However, as Parsi tradition places the latter under the reign of Shâpûr II., there can be little doubt of their identity.

2) See the Zand-Pahl. Gl. pag. XXXIII. 6. He is also mentioned in the proclamation of Khosru Parviz, which I shall presently notice.

ordered a Pahlavî translation of the whole Avesta to be made, we should certainly find so important a fact mentioned in the Pahlavî books. In a very long proclamation of Khosru Parvîz [1]) (A. D. 531—579), in which all the efforts of former kings, for the preservation and study of the Avesta, are mentioned, no translation is spoken of, though he would hardly have omitted to notice the fact, if any translation had been ordered to be made. The following is a translation of the more important part of this proclamation, bearing upon the history of the fate of the Zoroastrian writings [2]) :

1. 'Vishtâsp, the king, who was afflicted in consequence of his war with Arjâsp, ordered to collect every work which was composed in the language of the Magi, that the Mazdayasnian religion might receive help, in various ways, from all the knowledge which was in readiness; now came Arjâsp and the others, from outside (the kishvar) Qaniras (in which Iran is situated), to Frashôshtar, to inform themselves on the religion'. . . . .

2. 'Dârâi, the son of Dârâi, ordered two written copies of the whole Avesta and Zand, just as Zertohesht received them from Ormazd, to be preserved, one in the treasury of Shapîkân, and the other in the fortress of written documents (i. e. the archives)'.

---

1) It is contained in the Dîn-kart (vol. I. pag. 1—9 of my MS., and probably in the second part of the sixth book); my MS. begins in the middle of the proclamation, but that it was published by Khosru Parvîz, appears unmistakeably from pag. 7. lin. 1, where he introduces himself in the words: [Pahlavi script] 'I (liûman, see the index s. v. ragôman) Khosrû, the king of kings, descendant of Kavât'. He has previously mentioned several of the former rulers of Iran, as detailed in the text; and as none of his successors are mentioned, the proclamation can hardly be later than his time.

2) The Pahlavî text will be found in the appendix to this essay. As the translation is made from a single MS., and without the assistance of any Pâzand commentary, it is not very literal in the more obscure passages; but it gives the general meaning of the original.

3. 'Valkhash (Vologeses), the descendant of Ashkân, ordered that the whole of the Avesta and Zand, as they had come down in their purity, whatever fragments thereof had escaped the destruction and ravages of Alexander and the Roman (i. e. western) soldiers in the Iranian country, and remained partly in writings, and partly in oral tradition, with the Destur (Desturs), should be searched for, in each town he came to, and taken possession of, for the emperor [1]) (i. e. for the imperial library)'.

4. "'He that was Artakhshatr, the king of kings, the son of Pâpak, in order to obtain correct decisions (in religious matters), summoned Tosar, with all (the sacred books) that were scattered about, to his residence; when Tosar came, him alone he accepted, and the rest of the Desturs he dismissed. And he issued this order: 'All that may be obtained of the Mazdayasnian religion (religious books), differing from what is now (recognized) as knowledge and wisdom, in future does not exist for us (i. e. is not acknowledged)".

5. 'Shahpûhar, the king of kings, the son of Artakhshatr, ordered to collect again the non-religious writings on medicine, astronomy, and the investigations on time, place and quality, creation, existence and growth (i. e. philosophy), on the observance of religious orders, documents and other records and (literary) means, which were scattered in Hindûstân, Rûm and other lands, and to put them again together with the Avesta, and to present a correct copy of all this, to the treasury of Shapîkân; and it was taken (there), to show it to all those who were not dead, to enlighten them on the Mazdayasnian religion'.

6. 'Shahpûhar, the king of kings, the son of Auharmazd, collected all the sayings of the inhabitants of all parts of the earth, for enlightenment and investigation, in order to adorn the Apân Khânak (?). After Atrô-pât had purified the sayings (of Zertohesht) which were compared with all those of different creeds, the Nosks were counted (their

---

1) I read *shatruyâr*, 'emperor', instead of *shatruîhâ*, 'cities', in the Pahlavi text.

number fixed); and to those who were not dead (the Zoroastrians), he (Shahpûhar) thus said: 'Now since we have seen the religion (religions) in the world, no one should leave the other (each should keep to his religion); this I endeavour much to bring about".

From this important document, we learn that various Persian rulers of three different dynasties, the Achæmenian, Arsacidan and Sasanian, took an interest in preserving the Zoroastrian books, which are generally called Avesta-Zand, and in collecting the fragments and restoring the sacred writings to their primitive purity, after they had become scattered. But nowhere do we find a translation into the vernacular language mentioned. It is however stated that king Darius (II. or III.), the descendant of Darius (I. or II.), had two copies of the Avesta and Zand prepared. Now we know, from the Zand-Pahlavî Glossary 3, 6 (see also ind. s. v. *zand*, pag. 239—240), that *Zand* denoted the Pahlavî language; for the expression 'Avesta and Zand' means only the original text, with its commentary in the Pahlavî language. Hence arises the question whether the Pahlavî translations of the Vendidad, Yasna and Visparad, which we now possess, were actually composed *before* the Sasanian times. This must be answered in the negative, since it can be proved that they contain allusions to events which happened in those times, such as the appearance of Mazdak. Most probably, they were brought into their present form, in the sixth century A. D., during the reign of Khosru Parvîz who is said, in the Dîn-kart [1]), to have 'ordered the most intelligent and best of the Magian priests to make quite a new explanation of the Avesta and Zand'. This probably refers to the notes which are added to the translations, and now form part of them; for there can be no doubt that the bulk of the Pahlavî translation is founded on older versions, which had come down either from Arsacidan, or even from Achæmenian times. This is proved, not only from the considerable knowledge of Zand inflections, exhibited

1) Vol. I. pag. 7 of my MS.: 
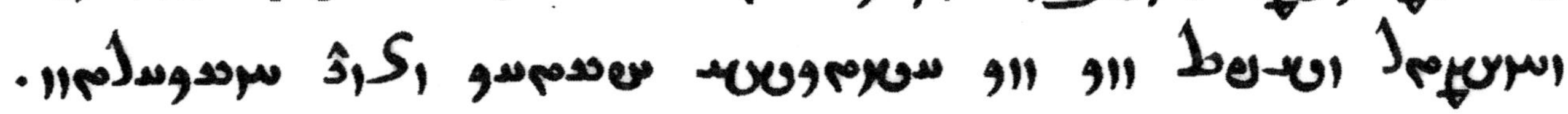

by the translation of the Vendidad, but also by passages in the translation of the Yasna, such as 30, 1., where both the Avesta and Zand are mentioned as scripture. Now the Zand, as we have seen, was the translation of the Avesta into Huzvâresh; and as we cannot suppose the translator was attributing the character of sacredness to his own work, we must conclude that he was referring to earlier translations, in this mention of Zand.

Appendix.

(A passage from the Dîn-kart, vol. I. pag. 4 — 5 of my MS., relative to the fate of the Zoroastrian writings down to the time of Shâpûr II., translated in pag. 145—147).

1.

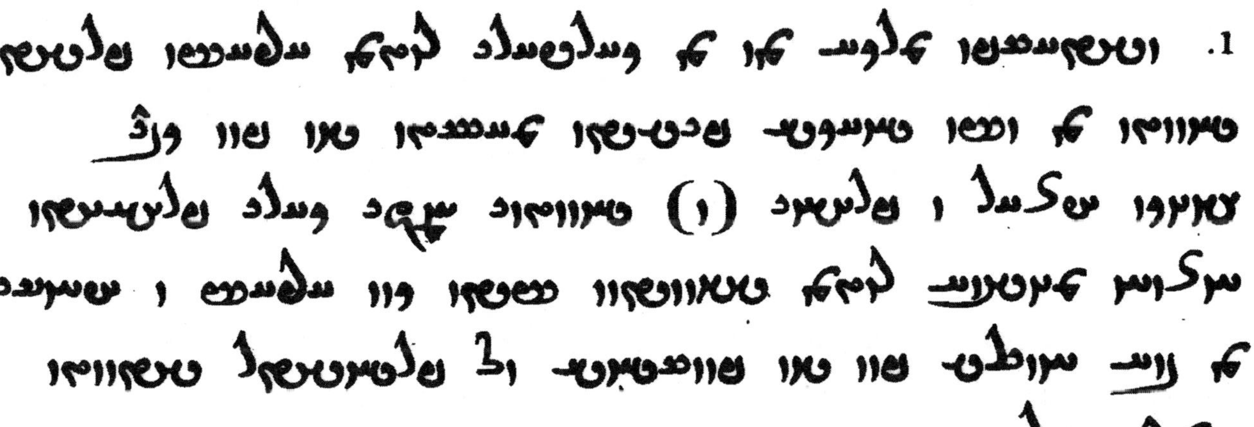

---

1. ***Veshtâspu malkâ, mûn men kârîzâr-i levatman Arjâspu faryâtu yehevûntu, men vespu dânâkîh pêsîtu mahîstu dînu pavan kabed ayinînaku afzâr va farhâng-i yehevûntu-i ham-chi kâr-i farhâkhtu huzvân magosîvâ levatman yakhsanûnîtanu sazîtu; kûn Arjâsp va avâr.k-i men barâ Qamîras, pavan dînu purseshnîh, val Frashôshtar yâtûntu hûmanand; sapar âkâsyêsh vîsh-i kartu.***

2. [illegible]

3. [illegible]

4. [illegible]

---

2. *Dârâi-i Dârâyân, hamâk Avestâk va Zand, chigûn Zartûhashtu men Auharmâ patîraftu, va napeshtaku 2 pechînu, khaduku pavan ganju-i Shapîkânu, khaduku pavan dazu-i napeshtu, dâshtanu farmûtu.*
3. *Valkhash-i Ashkânân, Avestâk va Zand, chigûn avîzakyêsh yîn yâtûntu yekavîmûnâtu, hamuku-chi afash konâ maman men vazand vâshuftkârîh-i Alaksandar va asvâr va rûpu-i Arûmâgân, yîn Aîrân shatru pôrgandakyêsh madam napeshtaku vad maman huzvân avascpardânîk pavan dastûbar katrûntu yekavîmûnâtu yîn, shatru chigûn frâz matu yekavîmûnât, nekâs dâshtanu val shatruîhâ asbâtkâr kartanu farmûtu.*
4. *Valman-î-i Artakhshatar malkâânu malkâ-i Pâpakânu, pavan râstu dastûbarih, Tôsar zak-ach hamuku-i pargandak va hamâk val babâ bûnshûnast; Tôsar madam matu; zak-î khaduku frâz patîraftu va*

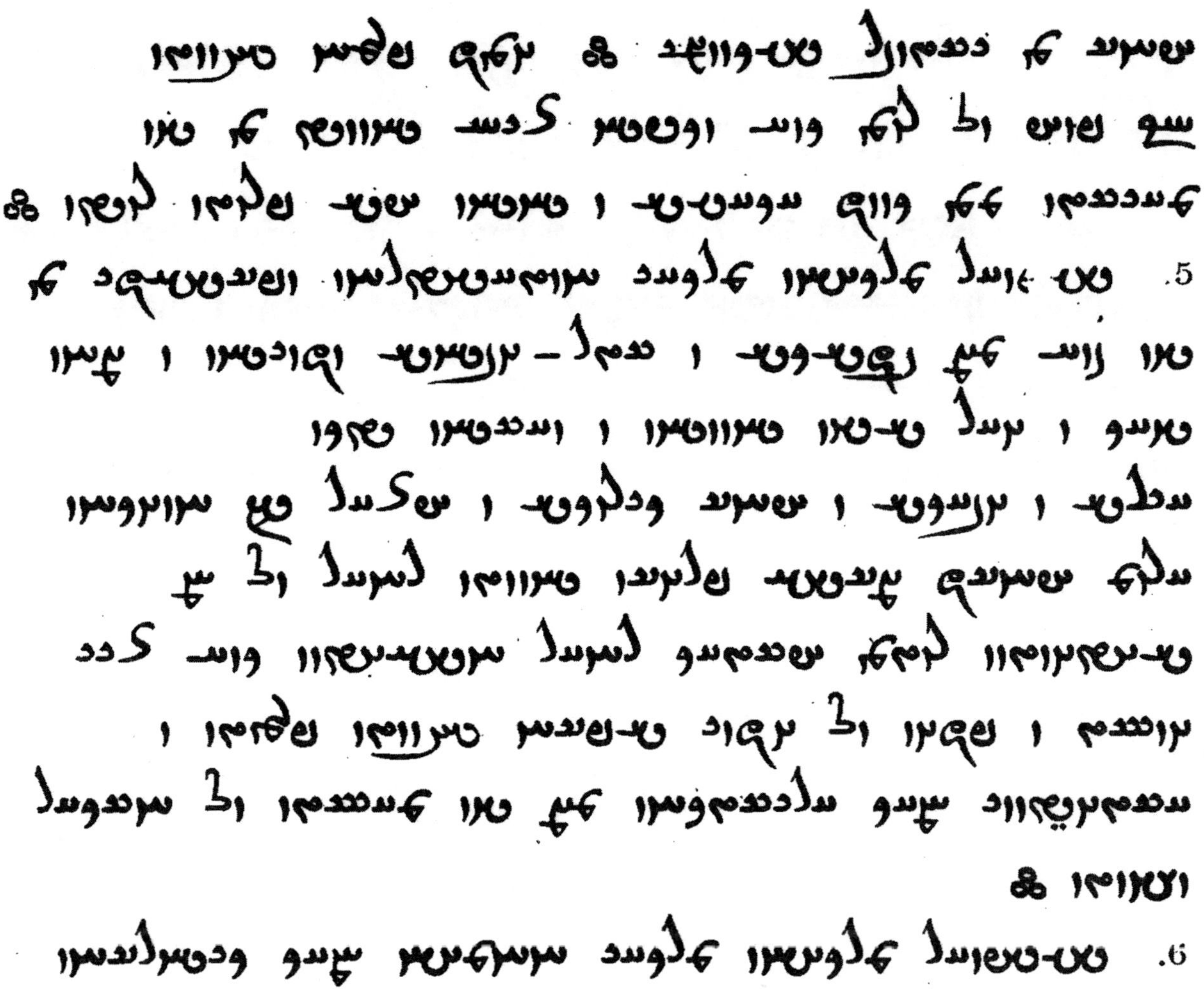

avârîk men dastûbar shîkûnyîn. Denman-cha farmân yehabûntu aîgh: frâz val lanman konâ nakîzeshn zakâi yehevûnêḍ, men dînu mahîstu maman kûn-cha âkâsîh va dâneshnu, afash farôtu lôîtu.

5. *Shahpuhar malkâânu malkâ-i Artakhshatarânu, napîkîhâ-ch-i men dînu barâ, madam bejashekîh va satar-gûbeshnîh, vajûîshnu va damânu, jînâk va gôhar, yakhsenon, yehevûneshnu va vakhseshnu, dataku aîrîh va gûbâkîh va avârîk kîrûkîh va afzâr, yîn Hendûkânu, Arûm, avârîk-cha damîkîhâ pargandaku yehevûntu, lakhvâr val ham yâîtyûntanu, levatman avestâk lakhvâr andâkhtanu, konâ zak-i durêst va pechînu val ganju-i Shapîkân yehabûntanu farmûtu; va khasetinîtanu-i hamâk arîstakânu madam dînu mahîstu val huskâr vakhdûntu.*

6. *Shahipuhar malkââanu malkâ-i Auharmazdân, hamâk kîshvarîkânu,*

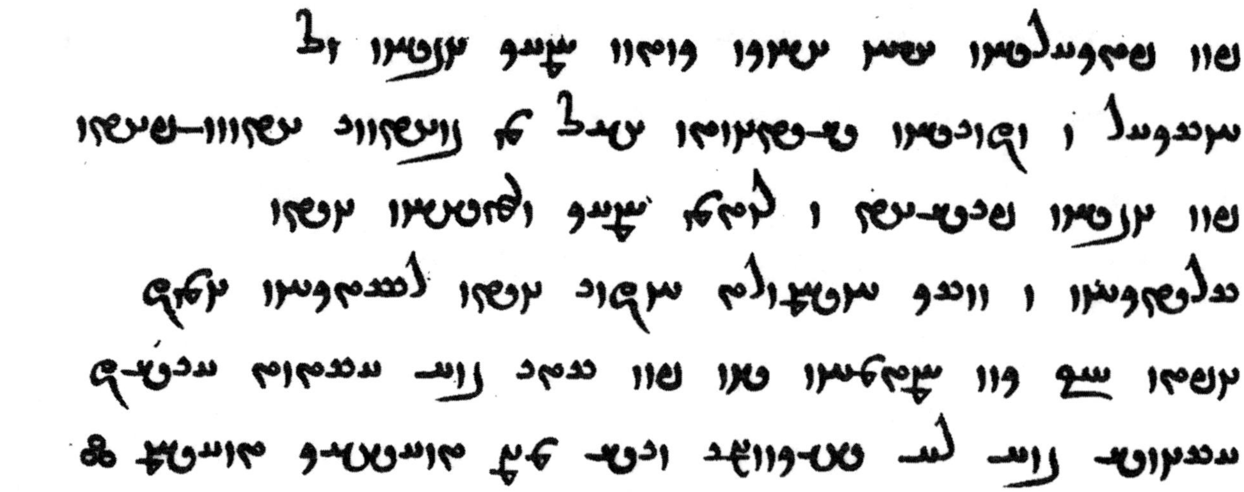

pavan patkâreshnu Avân Khânaku kartanu, hamâk gûbeshnu val huskâr va vajûîshnu yâîtyûntu, akhar men bûkhtanu-i Atôrô-pâtu pavan gûbeshnu pîshîd, va levatman hamâk valmanshânu javîḍu sarîḍakânu va nûsk hûshmûrḍ; anchu-i javîḍu rîstakânu denman-cha guftu aîgh: kûn amat-mânu dînu pavan sati barâ kheditûnt, aîsh-cha asyûnîh barâ lâ shîkûnyîn; vîsh madàm tukhshâk tukhshem.